5/20/70			
PEPL			
May 28/73			
July 3/73			

THE
VALENTINE
& ITS ORIGINS

ST. VALENTINE'S DAY

1. St. Valentine's Day in the Country, *The Graphic,* February 1870.

THE
VALENTINE
& ITS ORIGINS

FRANK STAFF

FREDERICK A. PRAEGER, *Publishers*
New York · Washington

BOOKS THAT MATTER

Published in the United States of America in 1969
by Frederick A. Praeger, Inc., Publishers
111 Fourth Avenue, New York, N.Y. 10003

Library of Congress Catalog Card Number: 69-12898

Printed in Great Britain

CONTENTS

INTRODUCTION

THE name of St. Valentine appears on calendars, but the Church does little to observe him, and it is in Britain and America, rather than on the Continent of Europe, that the memory of the patron saint of lovers has been kept alive.

Over the centuries, St. Valentine's Day has kept pace with the gradual change in social customs, and although fashion and the trend of events have sometimes allowed its observance to lapse, it has always been able to revive again; in more recent years this is doubtless due to the enterprise of greetings card manufacturers, who, by their efforts, have maintained the significance of this ancient holy day, symbolic of love and courtship.

Every year, too, as the 14th of February comes round, the traditions and customs of St. Valentine's Day are explained in magazines and papers. At this time, also, many museums arrange a special exhibit of old valentines which never fails to charm and please, and arouses nostalgic memories of the past.

Many valentines of the kind so keenly sought after by collectors today are veritable works of art; artistically assembled on hand-made decorated paper, they often reveal a beauty which can be seen nowhere else. Even when their artistic merit is questioned, they record for us a style and beauty belonging to an era to which we loosely apply the term 'Victorian'.

Long ago, when a valentine was made by hand, individuality, along with loving thought and care, went into its making, and no matter if the token of love was humble or simple in design, it was cherished equally as much as the one executed with dexterity and beauty; both kinds would nearly always be kept and treasured, and depending on circumstances would be handed down from one generation to the next, almost regarded as

heirlooms, and cherished out of sentiment and family association. Inevitably, as years go by, many of these old love letters and tokens become dispersed, some to find a new home among a collection of bygones, others to end up in a collector's album of valentines, to be admired and looked at by strangers.

It is inherent in man to collect—and everything is collectable; the collecting of old valentines has long been pleasurably pursued, and until quite recently, cards of exceptional merit could be found at comparatively little cost in antiquarian shops—often preserved in old family albums and scrap-books. They were so abundant that there seemed to be sufficient to supply the numerous collections in America, too, so that within the past twenty years or so many thousands of lovely old valentines have crossed the Atlantic to be treasured and admired in the very many fine collections there. This export of old valentines to the U.S.A. has now made the fine quarto-sized examples, which at one time used to be so plentiful, become quite scarce in Britain. Even rarer are 18th-century items which, because of their unusual size or shape, being so often in the form of 'puzzle purses', could not be conveniently displayed in an album, and so were among the first to disappear. There are many of these to be seen in American collections today, and, unless a place of origin is given on the valentine, it cannot be determined with any degree of certainty whether a particular specimen originated from Britain or from America. For, at that time, despite the great distance between them, customs and tastes of both peoples were very similar; the interesting exception is those designed in the Pennsylvania German *fraktur* style.

When gathering information for this book I often

heard of the old customs which continued to be handed down by word of mouth. Not long ago when visiting an old couple in a Devonshire village, I was told by them of the pretty custom of giving a pair of gloves on St. Valentine's Day, which they remembered. A few days ago the story was told me how in the country districts of Norfolk children are given little packets of sweets, delivered at the door secretly and by way of surprise, on St. Valentine's Day, a custom which is seemingly still being maintained and for which no adequate explanation is known.

Quite recently, on the bus journey from Boston, Mass., to New Haven, the youth I was sitting next to informed me that the custom of taking Valentine's names out of a box took place in the school he went to in a small town in North Carolina. This is surely a very modified form of the age-old custom, long since discontinued in Britain, when names would be 'drawn for' out of a box on St. Valentine's Day.

My story explains how valentines originated, and in writing it I am indebted to many people who have very willingly given me their help, particularly to Mrs. La Vaughn Wangler, consultant of the Hallmark Historical Collection in Kansas City, Mo.; to Miss Esther Mooney, the custodian of the Norcross collection in New York and to Mrs. Lillian Thrussell of the John Johnson collection at the University Press in Oxford. All these ladies have patiently attended to the many queries I put to them.

I am grateful also to Mr. Heany of the Rare Book Department of the Free Library of Philadelphia; Mr. Quimby of the Winterthur Museum, Delaware, and to those who helped me in the American Antiquarian Society of Worcester, Mass., and the Metropolitan Museum of Art, in New York. Also to Mrs. Sally Kington of the London Museum and Mr. Skeat of the Department of Manuscripts at the British Museum; Mr. Patterson, curator of the Castle Museum, York; Mr. Moseley of the St. Bride Printing Library, London; Mr. Pink of the University Library, Cambridge, and Mrs. Farrugia of the Post Office Records, G.P.O., London.

I owe very special thanks to Mr. Carroll Alton Means of Connecticut, who provided me with a great deal of unusual information and who has contributed the account of Jonathan King—"The Collector *par Excellence*"—as given in the appendix of this book.

My thanks also to the following who have all gone out of their way to help me in one way or another: Dr. Mario Nobile of Rome; Kate Gregory of New York; W. Bonwitt of London; Roland Knaster of London; A. R. Alcock of Cheltenham; R. A. Smith of Bath; Hayward Parrott of Aylesbury; P. Withers of Reading; P. F. Hinton of Sutton Coldfield, and Norman Eyre of Coventry.

West Bay, Bridport (Dorset) FRANK STAFF.
April 1968

2. Casket containing bones of St. Zenone and St. Valentine in the church of St. Praxedes in Rome.

THE ORIGINS

ANCIENT CUSTOMS AND TRADITIONS—THE FESTIVAL
OF THE LUPERCALIA—ST. VALENTINE

SENDING a valentine card on February 14 is no longer the serious matter it once was, and today is just a harmless and sometimes amusing way of keeping in touch with friends towards whom is felt an especial fondness.

In Britain and America the majority of people who use this means of saying "I love you" do so not only out of genuine sentiment but often for innocent amusement, and have no idea that the Saint's Day they are celebrating is connected with ancient customs which can be traced back to pagan times.

In all countries where man has lived for countless generations, superstitions and old customs become such a part of the life of the people that they are accepted without being questioned as to their reason or origins. Britain is rich in traditions and customs, and because the history of North America is linked with Britain's, some of these customs have been introduced into the United States.

For example, Hallowe'en—in ancient times a festival associated with fire and the supernatural—is today celebrated in some parts of America by children dressing up and parading through the streets carrying torches and lanterns, whilst illuminated pumpkins decorate the windows of houses. In Cornwall, the Helston 'Furry' dance is probably a survival of the *Floralia* celebrated by the Romans in honour of the goddess Flora, and some authorities claim that this ancient Cornish custom was a Spring festival long before the Roman occupation. The origins of the Mummers' plays are so ancient as to be untraceable, but obviously they depict a ritual of death and resurrection. Curious games of football in the streets, egg-rolling and the giving of Easter eggs, beating the bounds, wassailing apple-trees (still carried out in parts of Devonshire and Somerset) and many other quaint customs serve to remind us of our links with pagan times.

Nursery rhymes, too, have survived to remind us of events in our history when it was neither prudent nor safe to repeat personal opinions about those in authority, or on politics, and especially on religion—which is why we recite to our children today quaint little verses, which might seem to be nonsense. When we repeat the ancient rhyme "Mary, Mary, quite contrary"—we are referring to Mary Tudor, who was contrary to the Protestant faith. "Baa, baa, Black Sheep, have you any wool? Yes, Sir, Yes, Sir, three bags full, one for my Master, and one for my Dame, but none for the little boy who lives down the lane" is a political reference to questionable dealing in the wool trade, where the 'master' and the 'dame', i.e. the king and those in authority got the lion's share of the profit, with nothing at all for the people. Little Jack Horner is supposed to refer to a John Horner who benefited as a result of the dissolution of the monasteries in the time of King Henry VIII, by buying lands in the manor of Mells in Somerset. But this reference too, is misleading, because there is evidence of a still older jingle of a similar theme dating back to the 14th century.

It is therefore easy to understand how the origins of customs dating to the time when the Romans occupied the British Isles are obscure. One of these ancient customs concerns a Roman priest (*see* Appendix I, page 122) who was cruelly martyred outside the gates of Rome close to where is today the busy Piazza del Populo, and we might well ask ourselves why English-speaking peoples in different parts of the world perpetuate the memory of Saint Valentine in the way they do, for

9

3. A page from a copy of Chaucer's *Parlement of Bryddes* made in the early part of the 15th century, which shows the colophon with a roundel preceding the last stanza. Courtesy of University Library, Cambridge.

Valentine, known to be a very chaste man, was never in his life concerned with cupids and hearts, the mating of birds, or with lovers.

Valentine, according to Alban Butler, in his *Lives of the Saints*, was:

a holy priest in Rome, who, with St. Marius and his family, assisted the martyrs in the persecution under Claudius II. He was apprehended, and sent by the Emperor to the Prefect of Rome, who, on finding all his promises to make him renounce his faith ineffectual, commanded him to be beaten with clubs, and afterwards to be beheaded, which was executed on the 14th of February, about the year 270. Pope Julius I is said to have built a church near Ponte Mole to his memory, which for a long time gave name to the gate now called Porta del Popolo, formerly Porta Valentini. The greatest part of his relics are now in the Church of St. Praxedes.

It is obvious that there is nothing in this description to explain why he comes to be associated with our present-day celebration of the day of his death, February 14, and it can be stated at once that this connection of his name with that of love is purely accidental. Indeed, there is proof of other associations appertaining to Valentine which would seem at one time to have been quite as generally ascribed to him. During his lifetime it is said that he was subject to fits of epilepsy, so that after his death it was believed that, having experience of the disease, he would be the likely Saint to take an interest in epileptic sufferers. In some parts of Germany epilepsy used to be known as Valentine's sickness, and also as Veltins-Dance (in just the same way as St. Vitus's Dance is known for a particular type of illness).

In a translation from Naogeorgus' *Popish Kingdom* (1570), it is quoted:

Saint Valentine beside to such as do his power despise
The falling sickness sends, and helps the man that to him
cries.

Burton, in his *Anatomy of Melancholy*, referring to the practice of seeking the aid of the saints for the cure of 'melancholy' and diseases of the mind, lists a number of saints with the diseases for which they were the patrons, and mentions Valentine for "the falling sickness". A French Almanac of 1672 also associates St. Valentine's day in this way:

Du 14 Fevrier, qui est le propre jour Sainct Valentin on souloit dire —

Saignée du jour Sainct Valentin
Faict du sang net soir et matin;
Et la saignée du jour devant
Garde de fièvres en tout l'an.

Shakespeare's friend, Ben Jonson, was obviously averse to Saint Valentine's connection with lovers, for, referring to him in *The Tale of a Tub* he says that Valentine:

Left us example to do deed of charity,
To feed the hungry, clothe the naked, visit
the weake and sick, to entertain the poor,
And give the dead a Christian funeral;
These were the works of piety he did practise,
And bade us imitate; not look for lovers;
Or handsome images to please our senses.

But in spite of these references, it was as the Saint of Lovers that Valentine was to become known. How this came about was, as already mentioned, purely by accident.

One of the most important, as well as one of the most ancient, of the festivals celebrated by the Romans was the Lupercalia. This was a Spring festival involving peculiar fertility rites, and was especially concerned with young people. The following account from an old Roman history[1] is quoted for its interesting description.

The most ancient Order of the Priests were the *Luperci*, sacred to *Pan* the God of the Country, and particularly of Shepherds. They had their Name from the Deity they attended on, called in *Greek*, λύκαιος probably from λύκος a Wolf, in *Latin*, Lupus; because the chief employment of *Pan*, was the driving away such Beasts from the Sheep

[1] *Antiquities of Rome*, by Basil Kennett, London, 1776.

that he protected. The *Lupercalia*, as *Plutarch* observes, appears to have been a Feast of Purification, being solemnised on the *Dies Nefasti*, or Non-Court-Days of the month February, which derives its name from *februo* to purify: and the very Day of the Celebration was anciently called *Februarca*.

The Ceremony was very singular and strange.

In the first Place, there was a Sacrifice killed of Goats and a Dog. Then two Children, Noblemen's Sons, being brought thither, some of the *Luperci* stained their Foreheads with the bloody Knife, while others wiped it off with Locks of Wool dipped in Milk; the Boys must always laugh after their Foreheads had been wiped; This done, having cut the Goat-skins into Thongs, they ran about the Streets all naked but their Middle, and lashed all that they met in their Procession. The young Women never took any Care to avoid the Strokes, but rather offered themselves of their own Accord, fancying them to be great Helpers of Conception and Delivery. They ran naked, because *Pan* is always painted so. They sacrificed a Goat, because the same Deity was supposed to have Goat's Feet; which gave Occasion to his common Epithet of *Capripes*. As for the Dog we meet with in the Sacrifice, it was added as a necessary Companion of a Shepherd, and because of the natural Antipathy between them and Wolves.

Some have fancied with *Plutarch*, that these *Lupercalia* were instituted in Honour of the Wolf that preserved Romulus and Remus. Others carry their Original much higher, and tell us, that they were brought into *Italy* by *Evander*, before the Time of *Aeneas*.

[λύκαιος is an adjective rendered in Latin as *Lycaeus*, which relates to the Festival of the Lycaea, and took place at Mount Lycaeus in Arcadia. The term *Lycaea* was used by later Greek writers to denote the Roman *Lupercalia*, both words being ultimately derived from the word for 'wolf' in their respective languages. Lyceum, meaning a Temple of Love, has the same derivation.]

When the Romans invaded Britain, they introduced their religious festivals and customs, and in this way the festival of the Lupercalia was established in these Islands.

It is because Saint Valentine was martyred on the 14th of February, that his name has ever since been associated with the Spring festival of the Lupercalia, which took place on a fixed date, the 15th of February. For, in later years when the early Christian fathers were busy obliterating pagan superstitions and dates by substituting those of the Christian belief, names of many of the martyred Saints were used to replace the old festivals. In this way St. Valentine, having suffered on the eve of the Lupercalia, the 14th of February, was now to perpetuate for ever the memory of this festival of the return of Spring when "a young man's fancy lightly turns to thoughts of love" and when the birds begin mating. Centuries later it was usual on St. Valentine's Day for young men to draw by lot the names of young women, a custom that lingered in some of the more remote villages of the British Isles right up to Victorian times. Some accounts written during the Victorian era of St. Valentine's Day maintain that the putting of the names of young women into a box to be drawn for by the men was part of the ceremony of the Lupercalia, and this has been repeated so often as to be believed true. But it has been authoritatively stated that this has yet to be proved.[1]

During the early part of the last century it was customary in many parts of Hertfordshire on the 14th of February for the poor and middling class children to assemble into procession and go to the houses of the principal people of the place who would throw to them wreaths of flowers and true-lovers' knots. Two or three girls would then select one of the youngest boys in the party and deck him gaily with the garlands, placing him at their head. As they went on their way, they would sing:

> Good morrow to you, Valentine;
> Curl your locks as I do mine,
> Two before and three behind,
> Good morrow to you, Valentine.

Halfpennies would be thrown to them when they stopped before windows repeating this rhyme. Early in the morning, on St. Valentine's day, at Upwick, not far from Bishop's Stortford, troops of small children would wend their way from one house to another, chanting outside the windows "Tomorrow is come, Tomorrow is come"—and going on their way when halfpennies were thrown to them.

Formerly it was customary for girls in Derbyshire to first peep through the keyholes of the house doors before opening them on St. Valentine's Day. If a cock and a hen were seen in company it was regarded as a good luck omen for the peeper to be married that year.

In Northamptonshire the children of the villages used to go in groups, stopping before each house to repeat a salutation in verse.

Trivial as these anecdotes may sound, and today no longer practised and mostly forgotten (although still vaguely remembered by older country people), they can very likely be attributed to the ancient Lupercalia.

The well-known Painswick Feast, although celebrated on a Sunday in September, might also be a lingering memory of the Lupercalia. After a procession through the streets, the children join hands right around the church and, in the fashion of old country dances, advance and retreat three times. Some of the Painswick people bake 'puppy-dog pies' on this day—which traditionally are said at one time to have been made of real puppies—but since have been replaced by a round cake topped with almond paste with a little china dog inside. Remembering the sacrifice of a dog as part of the Lupercalia rites, and the fact that Painswick was a Roman settlement with a military camp nearby, this connection is not unreasonable.

The origin of the use of the word 'wolf' in connection with love is lost in obscurity, but it is probable that there is a connection between the Greek word *lykos*, meaning wolf, with the word lechery; also with the verbs *lécher* (Fr.) and *lecken* (Ger.) (Old Teutonic *likkôn*) and licentious. It is interesting to remember that the famous story of Romulus and Remus is not fictitious, for Faustulus, the shepherd who found the two baby boys at the bottom of a tree by the banks of the river Tiber, brought them to his home, where his wife Laurentia cared for them, nursed them and brought them up with his own children. Laurentia had formerly been a 'fallen woman' —a woman of the streets, called in Latin, Lupa, meaning a she-wolf.[2]

In ancient Pompeii, the little street called the Vicoli dei Lupenare was the *bordello*, and is now one of the attractions shown to tourists.

Today we still refer to one who fancies himself with the ladies as something of a 'wolf', and when a pretty girl walks down the street, young men give a 'wolf's whistle', which shows that the spirit of the Lupercalia is still with us.

[1] *See also* page 18.
[2] The popular legend is still perpetuated in Rome today by a pair of wolves kept in a cage beneath the Capitoline Hill.

THE EMERGENCE OF THE VALENTINE

CHAUCER AND THE MATING OF BIRDS—THE
PASTON LETTERS—16TH AND 17TH-CENTURY
REFERENCES—SAMUEL PEPYS

WHEN the Romans withdrew from Britain in A.D. 407 they left behind a Roman way of life, but without the Roman soldiers for protection; the early British peoples had a terrible struggle to survive, and for centuries afterwards endured the hardships and sufferings forced upon them through repeated invasions by Scandinavian and North German hordes.

By the memory of old beliefs handed down by word of mouth and through the influence of the Church in conserving so many of them, old customs and traditions survived, and after the Norman conquest another name comes to be associated with Valentine—Galantine. This is believed to be a Norman name, and, with a little knowledge of the origins of alphabets and words, it can easily be seen that one is nearly the same as the other. For, in our ancient language, *V* and *W* are the same, and *W* and *G* are the same; for example, Hugh is the same as Hew, and Plough is the same as Plow (bearing in mind

that the final *h* in both words is aspirate). Likewise, William is the same as Guillaume, and Norway is the same as Norge; and there are other similar examples. So that by a simple equation, *V* is the same as *G*, and Valentine can be accepted as Galantine. Whether this Norman word derives from St. Valentine will be hard to determine. In Victorian times, chroniclers of the word Galantine in connection with the Valentine story explain it as deriving from *Galant*, implying Gallant or Lover. This reference, however, must be regarded as extremely vague and uncertain, and might well be irrelevant, for the earliest written references which we have about St. Valentine's Day are all concerned with the mating of birds. It was a popular belief in the mediæval mind that around the middle of February was the time for birds to pair (and according to the 'Old Style' calendar, this would fall a little later in the year than now). It was also perfectly reasonable to suppose that this natural event

4. The 45th stanza from Chaucer's *Parlement of Bryddes*, or *the Assembly of Foules.* This early 15th century manuscript copy contains the earliest known written reference to St. Valentine's Day. Probably written about 1370-80 by Chaucer (who died in 1400). Courtesy of University Library, Cambridge.

13

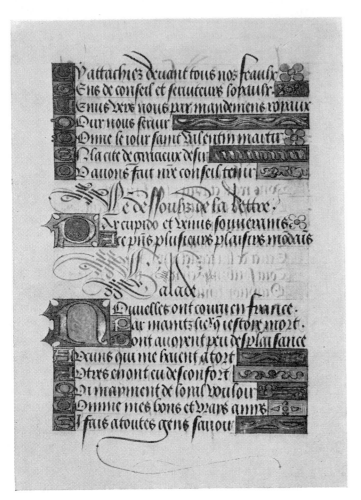

5. Verses by Charles, Duke of Orleans, showing the reference to Saint Valentine mentioned on page 15. Courtesy of the Trustees of the British Museum.

should also apply to human beings, so that St. Valentine's association with the spring-time mating of birds came to be regarded in the same way for lovers.

A charming description of St. Valentine's connection with birds is given in the 45th and 46th stanzas of Geoffrey Chaucer's *Parlement of Bryddes, or the Assembly of Foules*:

> For this was on Saint Valentine's Day
> When every fowl cometh to choose his make, (mate)
> Of every kind that men think may;
> And that so huge a noise gan they make,
> That earth and air and tree and every lake
> So full was, that underneath was there space
> For me to stand, so full was all the place.

---

[1] *Dictionary of Archaic and Provincial Terms*, Halliwell-Phillipps.

And right as Alain in the Plaint of kind
Deviseth Nature of such array and face,
In such array men might her there find.
This noble Empress, full of all grace.
Bad every fowl to take her own place,
As they were wont alway fro year to year,
Saint Valentine's Day to stonden there.

Towards the end of the poem, which describes at length the impatience of the birds to pair, and tucked between the two last stanzas, is a roundel:

> Now welcome summer, with thy sun soft,
> That hast this winter weather's overshake;
> Saint Valentine, thou art full high on loft,
> Which drivest away the long nights black
> Thus singen small fowls for thy sake;
> Well have they cause for to gladden oft;
> Since each of them recovered hath his make,
> Full blissful may they sing when they wake.

A little verse that was at one time believed also to be by Chaucer, but afterwards found to be of later date, the author unknown, describes a bright May morning, with the birds happily "tripping out of their bowers", and warbling in the joyfulness of the daylight.

> They pruned them, and made them tight gay,
> And danceden and lepten on the spray,
> And evermore two and two in fere.
> Right so as they had chosen them to year,
> In Feverere upon Saint Valentine's Day.

It is understandable that very little written evidence concerning St. Valentine could have existed prior to, and as far back as, the 14th century, so we are indeed fortunate in having what little mention there is. A curious little verse,[1] believed to be one of the oldest to give direct mention to the Saint, says:

> Thow it be alle other wyn
> Godys blescing have he and myn,
> My none gentyl Volontyn,
> Good Tomas the frere.

How, or under what circumstances, Friar Thomas came to be a Valentine we will never know, but the fact remains that he is recorded in this way in the oldest known 'Valentine' believed to exist.

14

Charles, Duke of Orleans, when imprisoned in the Tower of London after the Battle of Agincourt (1415), whiled away his time writing romantic verses. Most of them he wrote in the Norman French style, but some have come down to us in English, among them this very delicate poem with its allusion to Saint Valentine:

> The god Cupide and Venus the goddes
> Whiche power have on all worldly gladnes
> We hertly gretyng sende of oure humbles
> To louers alle
> Doyng you wite the duk that folkis calle
> Of Orlyaunce we him amylte and shall
> As oure servaunt which hath but yeris small
> Of youthe yit spent
> Gyve on the day of seynt Valentyn the martere
> As in the Castell of humbill desere
> As for the tyme oure counsell holdying here.

Another of his, when written in modern spelling, would not be out of place on one of today's valentine greetings cards:

> Wilt thou be mine? dear love, reply,—
> Sweetly consent, or else deny;
> Whisper softly, none shall know,—
> Wilt thou be mine, love? ay or no?
>
> Spite of fortune, we may be
> Happy by one word from thee;
> Life flies swiftly—ere it go,
> Wilt thou be mine, love? ay or no?

When later, during the 16th and 17th centuries, poets and song writers wrote profusely on St. Valentine's association with birds and lovers, their writings lead one to believe that the custom (so prevalent during the 17th century) of choosing one's Valentine was a traditional one that had always existed. John Lydgate, the Monk of Bury,[1] in a poem he wrote in 1440 in praise of Queen Catherine, consort to Henry V, stresses this point very clearly.

> Seynte Valentine, of custome yeere by yeere
>   Men have an usaunce in this regioun   (custom)
> To loke and serche Cupides Kalendere,   (look)
>   And chose theyre choyse, by grete affeccioun;
>   Such as ben prike with Cupides mocioun,
> Takyng theyre choyse as theyr sort doth falle:
> But I love oon which excellith alle.

At this time, choosing for oneself a Valentine was the same as being affianced; human beings paired together just as the birds did, and it would seem that St. Valentine's Day was the appropriate day to become engaged. Evidence of this is given in one of the Paston letters— that wonderful family correspondence which reveals so much of everyday mediæval English domestic life.

The Pastons were a large well-to-do family, who represented many aspects of English society. They lived in manor houses, and held estates in Norfolk and Suffolk, but essentially they were a Norfolk family. Their letters are rich in descriptions of country life: disputes over the estates, legal entanglements, personal opinions and all the worries and pleasures of everyday life are presented in detail.

In a letter written early in 1477, Dame Elizabeth Brews, the wife of Sir Thomas Brews of Stinton, Akenham, writes to her cousin John Paston, expressing the hope that he might contemplate marriage with their daughter, Margery. After touching on one or two matters of money, she says, "And, Cousin, that day that she is married, my father will give her 50 mark. But and we accord, I shall give you a greater treasure, that is, a witty gentlewoman, and if I say it, both good and vertuous, for if I should take money for her, I would not give her for a £1,000. But, Cousin, I trust you so much, that I would think her well beset on you, and ye were worth much more."

In February that same year, Dame Elizabeth wrote again to John Paston. In order to benefit from the richness and beauty of the old English, this extract, and the subsequent letters are quoted in the original text. Addressing her letter "to my wurschypfull cosyne, John Paston", she says:

> And, cosyn, uppon Fryday is Sent Volentynes Day, and every brydde chesyth hym a make; and yf it lyke yowe to come one Thursday at nyght, and so purvey yowe, that ye may abyde there tyll Monday, I trusty to God, that ye schall so speke to myn husband; and I schall prey that we schall bryng the mater to a conclusyon, &c., for, cosyn It is but a sympill oke That (is) cut down at the first stroke.

Encouraged by her help in this matchmaking, and pleased with his prospects, John Paston proposed to

---

[1] The original is in the British Museum: MS. Harl. No. 2241.

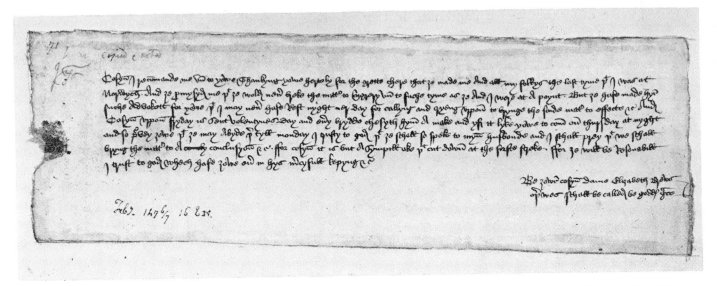

6. The letter written by Elizabeth Brews to her cousin John Paston, inviting him to come and visit, to meet her daughter, Margery, as, "Friday is Saint Valentine's Day and every bird chooses him a mate. . . ." Dated February 7, 1477. Courtesy of the Trustees of the British Museum.

Margery, and later that month she wrote to him, addressing her letter:

> Unto my ryght welebelovyd Voluntyn,
> John Paston, Squyer, be
> this bill[1] delyvered . . .

Ryght reverent and wurschypfull, and my ryght welebeloved Voluntyne, I recomande me unto yowe, ffull hertely desyring to here of yowr welefare, whech I beseche Almyghty God long for to preserve un to Hys plesur, and yowr herts desyre. And yf it please yowe to here of my welefar, I am not in good heele of body, nor of herte, nor schall be tyll I her ffrom yowe:

> For there wottys no creature what peyn that I endure,
> And for to be deede, I dare it not dyscure.   (discover)

And my lady my moder hath labored the mater to my ffadur full delygently, but sche can no mor gete then ye knowe of, for the wheche God knowyth I am full sory. But yf that ye loffe me, as I tryste verely that ye do, ye will not leffe me therefor; for if that ye hade not hafe the lyvelode that ye hafe, for to do the grettest labur that any woman on lyve myght, I wold not forsake yowe.

> And yf ye commande me to kepe me true and wherever
> I go,
> I wyse I will do all my myght yowe to love and never
> no mo.

> And yf my freends say, that I do amys,
> Thei schal not me let so for to do,
> Myne herte me bydds ever more to love yowe
> Truly over all erthely thing.
> And yf thei be never so wroth,
> I tryst it schall be better in time commyng.

No more to yowe at this tyme, but the Holy Trinite hafe yowe in kepyng. And I besech yowe that this bill be not seyn of none erthely creatur safe only your selffe, &c.

And thys letter was indyte at Topcroft, with full hevy herte, &c.,

> By your own
> MARGERY BREWS

This charmingly composed letter was then followed by another in which Margery alludes to the rather small dowry her father is allowing her. She hopes that the question of the money will not be mentioned again, and that she will be accepted for what she is. She writes:

Wherefore, yf that ye cowde be content with that good, and my por persone, I wold be the maryest mayden on grounde; and yf ye thynke not yowr selffe so satysfyed, or that ye myght hafe mech mor good, as I hafe undyrstonde be yowe afor; good, trewe, and lovyng volentyne, that ye take no such labur uppon yowe, as to come more for that mater, but let it passe, and never more to be spokyn of, as I may be your trewe lover and bedewoman duryng my lyfe.

16

No more unto yowr at thys tyme, but Almyghty Jesus preserve yowe, bothe body and sowle, &c.

By your Voluntyne,

MARGERY BREWS

Margery married John Paston, and we know from her subsequent letters, which help to enrich this wonderful family correspondence, that the marriage was a happy one.

From these few references and quotations it is easy to see that St. Valentine's Day was accepted as an important day in the calendar and, having for so long been associated with the mating of birds, was now connected with courtship and lovers, and especially with the choosing of a Valentine, or sweetheart, as the name had come to mean. This much is seen very clearly over the next two centuries in the many romantic references which have come down to us in ballads and songs. George Turberville, who was celebrated for his sonnets wrote on the choice of his Valentine in 1567 :

With others I to choose a Valentine
Addrest myself : each had his dearest friend
In scroll ywrit, among the rest was mine.   (written)
See now the luck by lot that chance doth send
To Cupid's crew, mark Fortune how it falls,
And mark how Venus imps are Fortune's thralls.

The papers were in covert kept from sight :
In hope I went to note what hap would fall;
I chose, but on my friend I could not light
(Such was the Goddess will that wilds the ball).
But see good luck : although I miss'd the same,
I hapt on one that bare my lady's name.

In *Hamlet, Prince of Denmark*, Ophelia sings :

Tomorrow is Saint Valentine's day,
All in the morning betime,
And I a maid at your window,
To be your Valentine.

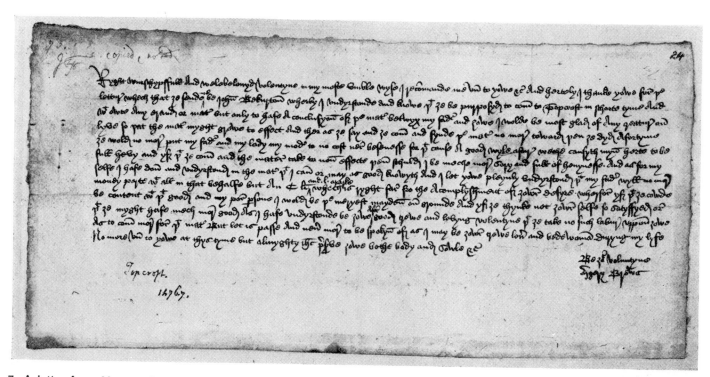

7. A letter from Margery Brews to her "Right Worshipful and well beloved Valentine" in which she explains, "Wherefore, if you could be content with that good, and my poor person, I would be the merriest maiden on ground; and if you think not yourself so satisfied, or that you might have much more good, as I have understood by you before; good, true, and loving valentine, that you take no such labour upon you, as to come more for that matter, but let it pass, and never more to be spoken of, as I may be your true lover and bedwoman during my life. . . .

By your Valentine,
Margery Brews."

This can be said to be the earliest known 'valentine', dated 1477. Courtesy of the Trustees of the British Museum.

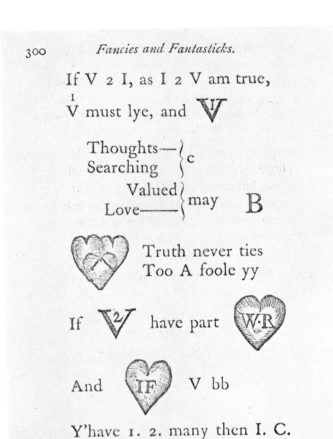

300 *Fancies and Fantasticks.*

If V 2 I, as I 2 V am true,

V must lye, and

Thoughts—
Searching
Valued
Love—— may B

Truth never ties
Too A foole yy

If have part

And V bb

Y'have 1. 2. many then I. C.
And R not worth
Write
I'le—— not yours VV

8. An early rebus of 1641, taken from *Witt's Recreations.* Courtesy of Carroll Alton Means, Connecticut.

Then up he rose, and donn'd his clothes,
   And dupp'd the chamber-door;
Let in the maid, that out a maid
   Never departed more.

By Gis and by Saint Charity,
   Alack, and fie for shame!
Young men will do't if they come to't;
   By cock, they are to blame.
Quoth she, before you tumbled me,
   You promis'd me to wed.

He answers:
So would I ha' done, by yonder sun,
   An thou had'st not come to my bed.

Robert Herrick, too, unrivalled for his beautiful lyrics composed a charming little poem to his mistress in 1648 beginning:

Choose me your Valentine,
   Next, let us marry; . . .

and wrote what is possibly one of his most delightful poems:

   To His Valentine, on St. Valentine's Day
   Oft have I heard both youths and virgins say
   Birds choose their mates, and couple too this day:
   But by their flight I never can divine
   When I shall couple with my Valentine.

Another appropriate verse occurs in *The British Apollo* (late 17th century):

   Why, Valentine's a day to choose
   a mistress, and our Freedom loose?
   May I my reason interpose,
   The question with an answer close?
   To imitate we have a mind,
   And couple like the winged kind.

The quotations are endless, and all stress the custom of choosing for oneself a Valentine on 14th of February, although reference is also made to the drawing by lot for one's Valentine.

This custom of drawing one's Valentine by lot is an ancient one, and is said to be a survival of one of the rites dating to Roman times, believed to have been part of the ceremony connected with the Lupercalia. It has been stated that the names of young women were put into a box and drawn for by the men, guided purely by luck. As already mentioned earlier, this supposedly Roman custom has been described and repeated on numerous occasions without any authority to substantiate it. There is no mention of it in any of the ancient references which describe the rites of the Lupercalia, nor is it referred to in the classic work, Smith's *Dictionary of Greek and Roman Antiquities.*

Connecting this custom with Roman times seems to have come about at some time during the Victorian era, when many articles were written on the subject of Valentine Day customs, and has so often been repeated that it has become accepted as a fact. Certainly it was common custom over the centuries in Britain to draw one's Valentine by lot and, the person, having become 'drawn', remained as Valentine for the whole year. Obviously, in many cases, this would lead to a betrothal. This much is vouched for by the many allusions given it in poems and ballads. In *Privy Purse Expenses of the*

18

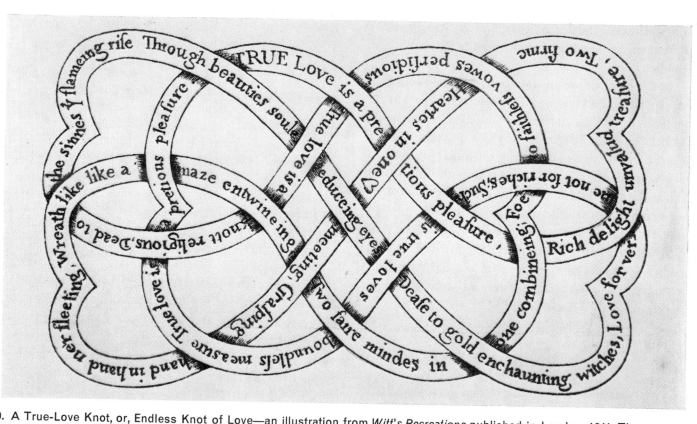

9. A True-Love Knot, or, Endless Knot of Love—an illustration from *Witt's Recreations* published in London, 1641. The message can be read at random from any line, and has neither beginning nor end. Courtesy of Carroll Alton Means, Connecticut.

Princess Mary (this is Mary Tudor who, unhappily, came to be known in later years as 'Bloody Mary'), there is an entry in February 1537-38: "Item, Given to George Mountejoy drawing my Lady's grace his Valentine," and on page 97 of the *Inventory of Jewels* mention is made of "a broach of gold enamelled black with an Agate of the story of Abraham with iii small rockt rubies", to which a marginal note says "given to Sir Antony Brown drawing her grace to his Valentine". These examples show that the custom prevailed among those who moved in good society and, as is often the case, little or no mention has been preserved of those people in a more humble station of life. For these we are dependent upon the reference made in the verses and ballads of those days. The last verse of one of Drayton's poems refers to the Valentine drawn by chance:

> Let's laugh at them that choose
> Their valentines by lot,
> To wear their names that use,
> Whom idly they have got.
> Such poor choice we refuse,
> Saint Valentine, befriend.

There were possibly many who were wearying of the custom, especially those whose intelligence rose above it, and the opinion of one, at least, is recorded to show the feelings of this sort of person. Dudley, Lord North, writing in 1645 to his brother, says: "A lady of wit and quality whom you well know, would never put herself to the chance of a Valentine, saying that she would never couple herself but by choice. The custom and charge of Valentines is not ill left, with many other such costly and idle customs, which by a tacit general consent we lay down as obsolete." Most certainly there were many times when chance was unfortunate in providing the wrong sort of partner, and to have to endure this kind of Valentine as one's special friend for one whole year must have been very trying.

However, the custom prevailed steadfastly, and it was not until Cromwell's time that the Puritans, as might be expected, abolished the observance of Valentine's Even (drawing by lot took place on the eve of the 14th of February)—along with Lammas Day, Whit Sunday, and all those fairs named after the saints, as well as Hallowe'en and Hogmanay night.

19

But, following the Restoration in 1660, St. Valentine's Day was remembered as ardently as formerly, with all the old customs revived.

It had long been customary to give a gift—and some of these, it has been noted, were often extravagant. At one time it was usual for both parties to exchange presents, but later, judging from the 17th-century references, it eventually became the custom only for the gentleman to offer a present. At first, the gifts were given at the time of drawing lots, but in later years they were given in much the same way as birthday gifts are today. Faithful accounts of this practice have been written by Samuel Pepys, who never failed to celebrate St. Valentine's Day. From remarks in his diary we learn that married as well as single persons were eligible as Valentines.

14th February, 1660. "My wife, hearing Mr. Moore's voice in my dressing room, got herself ready and came down and challenged him for her Valentine."

14th February, 1661. "Up early, and to Sir W. Batten's but I could not go in till I asked whether they that opened the door was a man or a woman; and Mungo was there, answered, a woman, which with his tone made me laugh; and so up I went, and took Miss Martha for my Valentine —which I do only for complacency; and Sir W. Batten he goes in the same manner to my wife, and so we were very merry."

In these two entries Pepys is referring to a much older St. Valentine's Day custom, where originally the first unmarried person encountered on the morning of the 14th of February became one's Valentine. In later years it was less seriously understood, until by Pepys's time it was merely a pleasant observance enjoyed amongst friends. But for all this, the custom lingered on in many country districts of Britain until well into the Victorian era, although usually observed by children and domestics.

This same custom was formerly carried on in France, where it is recorded as the most ancient custom connected with the Saint's day. In country districts, mainly in the eastern parts of France, the first young man to be seen by a girl on the morning of the 14th of February became her 'Valentin' or, in other words, her cavalier or boy-friend for the year. He was allowed to enjoy her company with the full consent of both families, and usually the friendship ended in a betrothal.

A few days after Pepys's St. Valentine Day entry, he wrote on the 18th February, 1661:

In the afternoon, my wife and I and Miss Martha Batten, my Valentine, to the Exchange, and there, upon a payre of embroydered and six payre of plain white gloves, I laid out 40s. upon her.

Mrs. Pepys was similarly rewarded by Sir W. Batten.

22nd February, 1661. "My wife went to Sir W. Batten's and there sat awhile, he having yesterday sent my wife half-a-dozen pair of gloves and a pair of silk stockings and garters for her Valentine."

This reference to garters and gloves is of more than passing interest, for we find them often mentioned in doggerel and verse, and several years later, even right into the Victorian era, gloves were to feature prominently as valentines. The following lines are typical of Samuel Pepys's time:

Blush not, my fair, at what I send,
'Tis a fond present from a friend.
These garters, made of silken twine,
Were fancied by your Valentine.
The motto, dictated by love,
Is simply—"Think on what's above."

And another 17th-century poem begins:

Go, little gloves, salute my Valentine,
Which was, which is, which must and shall be mine . . .

Samuel Pepys, in describing these St. Valentine's Day customs, has recorded not only his own feelings and thoughts, but also the experiences of all his contemporaries, and gives us therefore a very accurate picture of how people of his station behaved on that day. In reading his following year's entry, a slight note of annoyance is discernible, and we can well understand how the custom of drawing for one's Valentine by lot, although often amusing and pleasant for some, could be irksome for others.

14th February, 1662: "I did this day purposely shun to be seen at Sir W. Batten's because I would not have his daughter to be my Valentine, as she was the last year, there being no great friendship between us now, as formerly. This morning, in comes W. Bowyer, who was my wife's valentine, she having (at which I made good sport to myself) held her hands all the morning that she might not see the paynters that were at work in gilding my chimney-piece and pictures in my dining room."

We can imagine Mrs. Pepys's concern in avoiding one of the painters as her Valentine! A lady might be considerably embarrassed to receive a present from a gentleman whose attentions she had no wish to cultivate, but was compelled by custom to be his Valentine for that year. Although marriage can be said to be a lottery, the partnership is usually agreed to by both parties; but in the case of drawing for a Valentine, it was pure chance, and many would find themselves embarrassingly paired; it was consequently often prearranged that one's 'drawn' Valentine was the right one. Obviously, too, the charm of this age-old custom dwindled when one's pocket was touched, sometimes for a quite considerable amount, in the giving of a present to a person, merely because chance had decreed it. St. Valentine's Day was certainly a delight for the ladies who, having been drawn for a Valentine could expect a worthwhile gift by way of recognition. But it was not always a pleasure for the gentlemen who sometimes were compelled to give their gifts indifferently, by the luck of the draw, and this was probably one reason why the custom gradually lapsed, although continuing in a more moderate way. Pepys so often expresses his concern on how much his being drawn as a Valentine is going to cost him and describes so well his surprise on becoming one.

14th February, 1666. "This morning called up Mr. Hill, who, my wife thought, had come to be her Valentine, she, it seems, having drawn him, but it proved not. However, calling him up to our bedside, my wife challenged him."

15th February, 1666. "Mrs. Pierce by and by comes with my name in her bosom for her Valentine, which will cost me money!"

This reference to the carrying of a person's name drawn by lot is of interest—for it might signify the beginnings of the written valentine. Another similar and quite important reference occurs in Pepys's entry for the next year, which clearly presages the coming about of the written valentine.

14th February, 1667. "This morning come up to my wife's bedside—I being up and dressing myself—little Will Mercer to be her Valentine; and brought her name

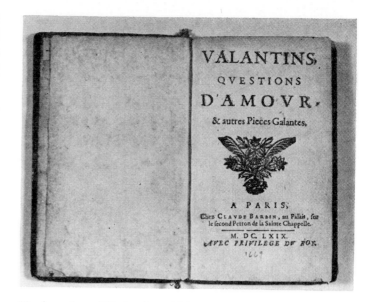

10. A curious little book on Valentines and Love published in Paris, 1669. Courtesy of Hallmark Historical Collection.

writ upon blue paper in gold letters, done by himself, very pretty, and we were both well pleased with it. But I am also my wife's Valentine, and it will cost me £5; but that I must have laid out if we had not been Valentines."

Here we have the very earliest recorded mention of a decorated hand-made valentine; and in his next entry is mentioned a new fashion when drawing for names—the novelty of drawing for mottoes at the same time.

16th February, 1667. "I find that Mrs. Pierce's little girl is my Valentine, she having drawn me, which I am not sorry for, it easing me of something more I must have given to others. But I do first observe the fashion of drawing mottos as well as names; so that Pierce, who drew my wife, did also draw a motto, and this girl drew another for me. What mine was I have forgot; but my wife's was, 'Most courteous and most fair;' which as it may be used, or an anagram made upon each name might be very pretty."

Indeed, in this effort of little Will Mercer (who was probably the small son of Mercer, Mrs. Pepys's maid) in making his "very pretty" valentine of gold letters on blue paper, along with the novelty of mottoes, and anagrams and word puzzles, we can perceive beginnings of what was to develop into the pictorial valentines of the next century, when they consisted not only of mottoes, with pictures and verses, but were beautifully and skilfully made to contain all sorts of surprises.

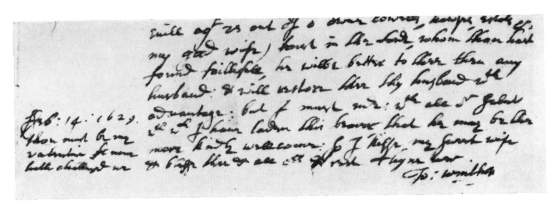

One of the few French references to this custom is contained in the accounts of the Court of Lorraine about the year 1630 where the cost is given of a present by Duke Charles III to the Duchess of Salm, who had become his Valentine.

Ruminating on the expenses of Valentines, Pepys relates that John Evelyn told him the Duke of York, being once the Valentine of the beautiful Lady Arabella Stuart, who he believed to be "as virtuous as any woman in the world . . . did give her a jewel of about £800; and my Lord Mandeville, her Valentine this year a ring of about £300". These amounts are indeed extravagant, and one may well wonder how much money was spent every year in this way, for it was certainly not unusual.

Later entries in Samuel Pepys's diary are mostly concerned with the cost of being his wife's Valentine, and we leave his journal with his further remarks on the expense of Valentines, believing that his concern was doubtless shared by many others in the Britain of those years.

14th February, 1668. "Up, being called up by Mercer (Mrs. Pepys' maid), who come to be my Valentine, and I did give her a guinney in gold for her Valentine's gift, There comes Roger Pepys betimes, and comes to my wife, for her to be his Valentine, whose Valentine I was also, by agreement to be to her so every year; and this year I find it likely to cost £4 or £5 in a ring for her which she desires."

15th February, 1669. "To my cosin Turners, where, having the last night been told by her that she had drawn me for her Valentine, I did this day call at the New Exchange, and bought her a pair of green silk stockings and garters and shoe-strings, and two pair of jessimy gloves, all coming to about 28s., and did give them to her this noon."

In this same year, 1669, a curious little book was published in Paris entitled *Valantins, questions D'amour et autres pièces galantes* (*see* Plate 10). It might well be that the writing of valentines and lovingly written notes was already fairly general, but little, if any, of this kind of bygone custom seems to have survived; there are no known examples recorded in the many private collections or in museums either in Britain or in America, as early as this. This is probably because, whereas the letters and papers of important and prominent personages have been cared for and preserved, those of ordinary people in more humble circumstances have been overlooked and allowed to be lost.

Such a letter, preserved in the library of the Massachusetts Historical Society, in the Winthrop Papers, is the one written by John Winthrop, the Governor of Massachusetts Bay Colony, to his wife, prior to his sailing from London for New England. Dated in 1629, it reads:

My sweet wife, The opportunity of so fitt a messinger, and my deepe engagement of Affection to thee, makes me write at this tyme, though I hope to followe soone after. The Lorde our God hath ofte brought us togither with comfort, when we have been longe absent, and if it be good for us, he will doe so still: when I was in Ireland he brought us togither againe: when I was sicke heer at London, he restored us togither again: how many dangers neer death hast thou been in thy selfe and yet the Lorde hath granted me to injoye thee still: if he did not watch over us, we need not goe over sea to seeke death or miserye, we should meet it at every steppe, in everye journey: and is not he a God abroad as well as at home? is not his power and providence the same in N england that it hath been in old England. If our wayes please him he can commande deliverance and safetye in all places, and can make the stones of the feild, and the beastes yea, the raginge seas and our verye enemies, to be in league with us. but if we sinn against him, he can rayse up evill against us out of our owne bowells, howses, estates, etc.

22

My good wife, trust in the Lorde, whom thou hast found faithfull, he wilbe better to thee than any husband: and will restore thee thy Husband with advantage: but I must end: with all our salutations with which I have laden the bearer, that he may be the more kindly wellcome: So I kisse my sweet wife and blesse thee and all ours, and rest Thyne ever

                           Jo: Winthrop

Feb. 14: 1629 Thou must be my
            valentine for none
            hath challenged me.

This affectionately written letter is of more than casual interest for, penned as it is in strongly puritanical style, it shows that Puritans too, as well as being sentimental were still remembering St. Valentine's Day.

Another very early reference is a valentine message dated October 25, 1684, written on the fly leaf of a small book, from which it has long ago become separated, to be preserved as a valentine. In this, the name 'Valentine' refers either to the person who was drawn as Valentine for that year, as was the custom, or was the betrothed of the person writing. This will explain why the date is other than the 14th of February.

    Goodmorrow Vallentine God Bless you ever
    Faithfull in promises, constant
             for ever

    Goodmorrow Vallentine
    God send you ever
    To keep your promise and
    be constant ever.
    (signed) Edward Sangon
            Tower Hill.   1684
            London   October 25

(The last verse is repeated between two scroll flourishes.) *See* Plate 12.

A little verse from *Poor Robin's Almanach* (an annual publication similar to *Old Moore's Almanach*, but compiled for amusement) in the February Calendar, and dated for 1670, has this to say about the drawing of Valentines:

    Young men and maids, where love combines,
    Each other draw for Valentines;
    They clip and kiss, and dance and sing,
    And love like unto anything:
    For young men they like to be doing.
    And freely spend their coin in wooing;

    And maidens love not to be tarrying,
    But make all haste they can to marrying;
    Yet oftentimes they find this measure,
    Marry in haste, repent at leisure.

And in the issue for 1684, alongside the column dated for February, is said: "and on the fourteenth day the Milleners will have great sale for gloves and ribbons".

The popularity and significance of St. Valentine's Day as a day to celebrate is proved by the enormous number of poems and lyrics which have been written. Endlessly they appeared from one year to the next, often composed by the best poets of the time along with those whose names were not so well known. In no other country can be found so many beautifully written verses touching on love and affairs of the heart in honour of St. Valentine as in the Britain of those times.

Mention and reference to St. Valentine customs in other countries are scarce. A 19th-century authority, Simrock, in his *Handbuch der Deutsche Mythologie*, states that England, northern France and the Netherlands were the special 'Valentine' countries. At one time, during the middle ages, Italy observed the 14th of February as a Spring festival and celebrated the occasion in the open air. Young people would gather in leafy glades and in ornamental gardens, where they would listen to recitals of amorous sonnets and verses; moved by the strain of romantic music both boy and girl Valentines paired off and strolled away together in the gardens. It was indeed a veritable *cour d'amour*.

But this pleasant custom did not remain in Italy, for according to enquiries which were carried out at the beginning of this century about the origins of Italian folklore and customs, it was found that no vestige of St. Valentine's Day celebration whatsoever has taken place in Italy for centuries. Much the same has happened in other countries. Both in Austria and in Hungary obscure courtship customs might be associated with St. Valentine's Day, and in Germany the day used to be celebrated, but the custom has long since disappeared.

Perhaps this can be attributed to the influence of several zealous pastors, who, according to Alban Butler, substituted Saint's names in the place of those of well-known men and women. He states how St. Francis de Sales[1] "severely forbad the custom of Valentines, or

---

[1] St. Francis de Sales (1567-1622), canonised in 1665. In 1923 he was adopted as the patron saint of journalists.

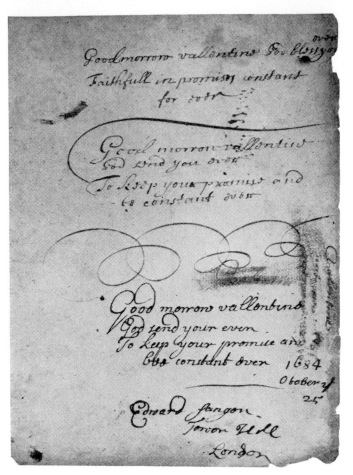

12. Written on the fly leaf of a book – this might have been a gift from a 'valentine', or it might be a few lines written in practice. It represents, nonetheless, an early, dated valentine souvenir. Courtesy of K. Gregory, New York.

giving boys in writing the names of girls to be admired and attended on by them; and, to abolish it he changed it into giving of billets with the names of certain Saints for them to honour and imitate in a particular manner". A definition of valentines given by one authority is: "in the Church of Rome, Saints chosen on St. Valentine's Day as patron for the year ensuing." But in the British Isles, the St. Valentine's Day custom continued to be observed, and also, to a limited extent, in some parts of France, where the 14th of February used to be highly honoured. It might well be that some of the customs, particularly those where 'drawing for' occurred, were introduced into France from Scotland.

One curious custom formerly used to take place in Corcières in the Hautes-Vosges. The elders of the commune having supposedly made suitable enquiries of those young people (as well as older unmarried ones) thought to be eligible for marriage, divided into two groups, each going into houses which faced one another in a narrow street of the town. Then, with the lower floor windows open, names of boy and girl Valentines would be called across from one window to the other, and in this way they would be paired, and carefully listed. Afterwards, when the couples were made acquainted with one another, they got together, and if satisfied with each other, the girl would prepare a tasty meal for her Valentine, who would bring with him a bottle or two of wine to celebrate the occasion: they would then finish the evening at a public dance. But if a young man did not care for the Valentine chosen for him, he would desert her. The poor girl would then stay alone for eight days, until, on the eve of the Sunday following the pairing, large bonfires would be burned in the middle of the village, when effigies of those who had spurned their chosen Valentines would be burnt—whilst abusive things would be called out about them.

But this kind of public 'drawing' for Valentines in France fell into disrespect, for it left too much opportunity for malice and ridicule. An old debauched man might be paired with a young coquette, just for fun. A married man, known to be loose with his moral obligations, would get himself publicly abused. So that in March 1776 the French parliament decreed that there would be no more calling and pairing of Valentines. But although suppressed, the idea lingered on, principally as a children's game, played with cards.

It is recorded that the Bishop of Metz was the first to take steps to prohibit these valentine customs as far back as 1737, but his measures took no effect. In February 1779 it was necessary for the police to issue public proclamations condemning these practices under penalty of a fine of 100 livres. Nevertheless, it appears that the custom was too firmly embedded in the people's minds, for, on February 14, 1806, the mayor of Metz was obliged to order the police to issue severe warnings to all who carried on the valentine traditions. Still the years rolled on, and the cries for 'Valentines' were heard in the streets of Metz, until new jurisdiction by the police in July 1816 eventually put a stop to them. Since that time, France has not celebrated February 14—or other traditions connected with St. Valentine. But as recently as 1912 any young man who rendered service to a lady, acted as escort to her, or accompanied her to a dance—who, in short, acted as her 'cavalier'—was termed her Valentine.

18TH-CENTURY DEVELOPMENT

CUSTOMS—LOVE-TOKENS AND TRUE-LOVE KNOTS
—RELIGIOUS VALENTINES—THE EVOLUTION OF
GREETINGS CARDS—GERMAN FRIENDSHIP CARDS
—PENNSYLVANIA GERMAN 'FRAKTUR' WORK—
EARLY AMERICAN VALENTINES
—18TH-CENTURY ENGLISH VALENTINES

FEW perceptible changes seem to have taken place in the St. Valentine's Day observances until about the middle of the 18th century, around 1760. By this time it was no longer the practice to give expensive presents to one's Valentine; instead, a love-token or a prettily written letter would be given. Otherwise the customs and traditions were still kept up, and romantic poems continued to be written in profusion. But the old ideas appear to have been carried on mainly by children, apart from those sentimentally inclined. It is thanks to children that so many of the old customs were saved from being forgotten, and in this way continued to be observed right up to the turn of this century. Some lingered on in the forms of games, such as 'kiss-in-the-ring' and other similar games where a form of elimina-

tion was present; others dwindled into card games, where 'pairing' or 'drawing' in some form or other was the order of play.

A learned French traveller, Misson, who died in England in 1721, has described a St. Valentine's Day custom as he saw it. Translated from the French, he says: "On the eve of the 14th of February, St. Valentine's Day, the young folks in England and Scotland, by a very ancient custom, celebrate a little festival. An equal number of maids and bachelors get together, each writes their true or some feigned name upon separate pieces of paper (billets), which they roll up, and draw by way of lots, the maids taking the men's 'billets' and the men the maids'; so that each of the young men meets with a girl whom he calls his Valentine, and each of the girls comes

13. A typical religious valentine delicately cut out of parchment. Note the figure 3 over a sacred heart, which was a symbol for faithfulness. Usually made by nuns, such items date about 1700-30. "And so mere chains can never bind the heart from love it's sure to find." Courtesy of the Hallmark Historical Collection.

14. *Far right.* A devotional valentine embossed and perforated on fine parchment, dedicated to St. Madeleine. Mid-17th century. Courtesy of A. R. Alcock, Cheltenham.

15. Visiting card, mid-18th century, engraved in green, with motif of Cupid and doves. Used as a New Year's Greetings Card. Author's Collection.

16. Danish, c. 1790–1800. Lover's card in the form of a transparency. When held to the light he is seen placing his heart at his sweetheart's feet. Author's Collection.

to a young man whom she calls hers. By this means each has two Valentines, but the young man sticks to the Valentine who has fallen to him rather than to the Valentine to whom he is fallen. The luck of the draw having thus divided the company into so many couples, the Valentines give treats and presents to their maids and wear their 'billets' over their hearts or on their sleeves. Sometimes a dance is arranged, and the little festival often ends in love. There is another kind of Valentine, which is the first young man or woman that chance throws in your way in the street, or elsewhere, on that day."

Throughout the 18th century, although presents continued to be given as formerly, usually by the gentle-men, in some parts of the country, especially in Scotland, the giving of valentine gifts was reciprocal and often in the form of a love-token or a true-love knot.

> The day Saint Valentine,
> When maids are brisk, and at the break of day
> Start up and turn their pillows, curious all
> To know what happy swain the fates provide
> A mate for life. Then follows thick discharge
> Of true-love knots and sonnets nicely penned.

Doubtless the high cost of postage is probably one reason why so few 18th-century valentine 'love-letters' are known. For, although a penny post existed in London, it was not until 1765 that a letter could be carried for one penny in country districts, and even so, only for the distance of the first stage of the post's journey, which would be about 15 miles, and the post at that time was either a foot post or mounted; letters were not carried by coach until 1784. Letters, being rated according to mileage and depending upon the number of sheets of paper, meant that the cost of sending a valentine through the post by a young man to his sweetheart was a luxury only available to those who could afford it. To a country lad, it could represent a week's wages or more, and as country lads usually found their maids in the same village, they would leave their love-tokens and valentines (as these love-letters became known) at their sweetheart's door.

In Wales, a love-token sometimes took the form of a spoon, and although not a Valentine Day custom, this old Welsh practice is worthy of mention. A young man when betrothed to a maiden would carve for her a spoon out of a piece of wood, using only his pocket knife. When finished it would be threaded on a piece of ribbon and worn around the girl's neck as a sign of the engagement. Sometimes, depending upon the ability of the carver, the spoon would be elaborately designed. From this custom we derive our word 'spooning', when applied to two people courting.

In Europe, and especially in German-speaking areas, where, with the exception of a few places, St. Valentine's Day was no longer observed, the exchange of gifts in the shape of love-tokens and lovingly written verses was customary. Not just for St. Valentine's Day, but for any appropriate day of the year. These take their place with what we now call valentines, for they served the same purpose, although not necessarily given on the 14th of February.

In Germany, too, it had long been the custom to use beautifully decorated baptismal certificates; these often depicted a heart, sometimes two, and in the case of marriage certificates, very often a man and maid standing before an altar would be shown. Alongside would be a hand-written message or verses tenderly or sometimes lovingly phrased. These so much resemble valentines that they are often mistaken for them, but it is probable that they have a direct bearing on the decorative and pictorial valentines which gradually came into being towards the turn of the 18th century.

Of the earliest forms of *Andachtskarten* (devotional cards), which closely resemble the pictorial valentines, are the little parchments which were obtainable in blank form to be made up as required. Dating from the early part of the 18th century, they were usually made up with delicate pin-prick and cut-out work and decorated by monks or nuns.[1] With a little picture of Holy Mary they invariably show somewhere in the design the Sacred Heart, and, remembering that the life work of St. Francis de Sales was devoted to the Order of the Sacred Heart, the connection can clearly be seen. In this way, the heart motif continued to be the main decoration on religious or devotional valentines and *Andachtskarten* of this sort, and came to be incorporated in the designs of other kinds of greetings cards and papers as the years went on.

Lovers' greetings were not at first written on cards, but on normal sized sheets of paper, and were commonly known as *Freundschaftskarten* in German-speaking countries. Subsequently they appeared written or printed on cards which had evolved from the ordinary greetings card of the period; this, in its turn had come about through the custom of writing short greetings messages on visiting cards (*see* Plate 15). It was about the middle of the 18th century that visiting cards were first published as such. Before this time, it had been a long established custom to write one's name on the blank side of a disused playing card. At first, printed visiting cards were usually embellished with a decorative border, sometimes very simple, the centre being left blank for the name to be written in; but as time went on, these little cards came to be printed pictorially, and

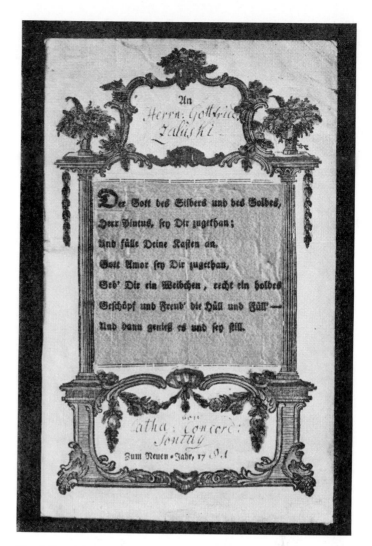

17. A New Year's card, 1781. German. Hand-coloured in green, pink and yellow, with gilded ornaments. The message, printed on red silk, says: "May the Lord Pluto, God of Silver and Gold, do you well; And fill up your coffers. May the God of Love do you well and give you a lovely little wife, Enjoy her to the full and be content." Author's Collection.

were sold in sets. They were sometimes designed by good artists who did not consider this sort of work beneath them. As well as being highly decorative they often depicted little views, the ruins and places of antiquity being very popular.

Around the New Year it was a Continental custom for people to call on friends and to leave their card, on which they had written a seasonal message, and in this simple way the greetings card habit evolved. Although the New Year was the popular date for this use, friends, especially lovers, would send to each other daintily printed cards bearing hand-written expressions of

[1] Similar work, known as *Spitzenbilder* and dating to the 15th century, is recorded by Max Bucherer in his book *Spitzenbilder: Papierschnitte, Porträtsilhouetten* (Einhorn Verlag, Dachau, Munich).

18. In typical fraktur-style, this Baptismal Certificate dated January 28, 1763, brightly coloured in red and other more subdued colouring, illustrates the sort of design which eventually became traditional for valentines. Courtesy of Henry Francis du Pont Winterthur Museum, Delaware.

19. Pennsylvania German. A fine example in fraktur style, and hand coloured. This delightful love letter, dated 1769, carries a puzzle message in the centre. Courtesy of the Free Library of Philadelphia.

20. This very fine hand-made valentine, drawn with pen and ink and water colours, is in the form of an acrostic and dates from about 1780. Courtesy of Norcross Collection, New York.

21. A True-Love Knot written in the shape of a labyrinth. American about 1780. Courtesy of the Free Library, Philadelphia.

22. Valentine in cut-out paper. One of the messages says: "The Rose is red, the grass is green, God bless you, the King and Queen." which could date it either 1820s or 1830s. Author's Collection.

endearment. From the improvised use of one's visiting card as a form of greeting to a card specially printed was a natural step (*see* Plate 17).

By the 1780s they were being published in every sort of style, showing a whole range of subjects, many having little winged cupids as the main design. About this time, cards, conforming to the usual size of a visiting card, were printed with New Year's greetings. Again, it is in Germany that they seem to have been most commonly used, examples seen dating from the 1770s. But in Paris, too, mention is made of this form of card in 1777. The printed Freundschaftskarten—friendship, or lover's cards—soon followed, which as a rule were affectionate and tender in style, and nearly resemble the valentine greetings cards of the next century. Today these Freundschaftskarten are avidly looked for by collectors, as early examples are extremely rare.

Freundschaftskarten emanated from Germany, along with decorated baptismal and marriage certificates, and it is easy to understand how those Germans, mainly from the Rhineland and others from the Low Countries, who settled in the United States during the 18th century introduced this particular form of greeting and style. It is known from the number of mementoes which have been so carefully treasured, dating from the 18th century, that St. Valentine's Day was as popularly celebrated as it was in the British Isles, having come over from Britain with other old customs; and several of these 18th-century love letters to be seen today in museums and collections, originate from places in Pennsylvania and are written in German, having been used by the Pennsylvanian German people who had settled there. Some of these early American efforts are considerably older than any similar decorated specimens known in England and, depending on the skill of the giver, vary a great deal in their style and decoration.

In style they conform more or less to the mediæval manuscript method of decoration, and take the name *Fraktur*, a German term used to describe the illuminated manuscripts with lettering based on the very early

29

23. Love Token c. 1800, Pennsylvania. Exquisite scissors work showing a double heart with initials E. R. Courtesy of Hallmark Historical Collection.

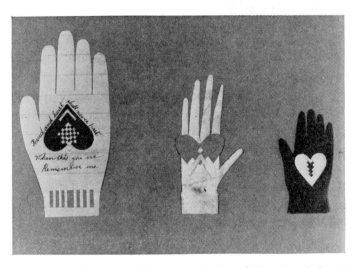

24. Hand-made Love Tokens, cut-outs of hand and heart motifs. Found in Suffield, Connecticut. Courtesy of Hallmark Historical Collection.

Gothic type face. It is therefore thanks to the Pennsylvanian Germans that this form of mediæval manuscript tradition has been preserved into the early part of the 19th century. Examples of this sort of work are to be found not only on the birth and baptismal certificates but also on religious broadsheets, on all sorts of written manuscripts with decorated borders, on *Irrgartens* (labyrinths in the form of puzzle pictures), on bookmarkers and bookplates, and other ornamental art of this nature, including valentines. Fraktur work nearly always shows interlace and stripwork and other similar ornamentation, and has come to be accepted by common usage as the most adequate way to describe Pennsylvanian German decoration usually drawn with pen and ink and brightly coloured.

Although these Pennsylvanian German people kept very closely to themselves, living in almost closed communities, this particular style of ornamentation certainly penetrated to other parts of the country, for valentines are found drawn in fraktur style, but written in English, from places far from their colonies which were largely centred in Pennsylvania.

25. Hand-drawn and coloured in red and blue showing the Endless Knot of Love against the background of a large heart, painted red, c. 1790–1800. Courtesy of Free Library, Philadelphia.

26. A well-designed puzzle purse, c. 1790. Including the front and back of the cover, the messages are contained within six panels. Courtesy of American Antiquarian Society.

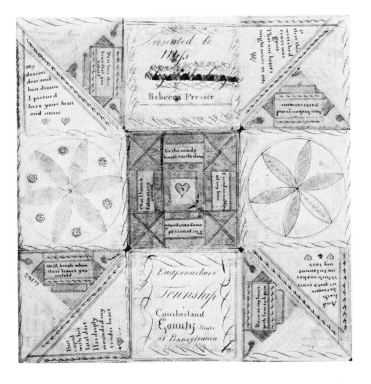

27. Valentine in the form of a puzzle purse, with concealed messages on both sides of the paper. Made in Eastpennsboro, Cumberland County, Pennsylvania, c. 1780. Courtesy of Henry Francis du Pont Winterthur Museum, Delaware.

No matter that some are rather crudely drawn, whereas others show a high standard of finish and exquisite penmanship, the loving care and painstaking work which was given to all of them show so very clearly the loving and tender thoughts that went with them. It is more than likely that this sort of work influenced the style of the decorated American valentine which was beginning to come into its own about this time.

A beautiful example of one of these is in the Norcross Collection in New York. Dated from Betschdorf in Pennsylvania in 1753, it is delightfully hand-decorated in typical Pennsylvania German style. Translated, it says:

> God and the Trinity planned the state of marriage. He told me also the vow which today I give to you, my little bird. If you become my wife, I will be faithful and dutiful, that good fortune and peace will flourish, and our home and wealth will profit by our work. This do I write you, my darling,
>
> Your faithful Philipp, in
> the year 1753

In this instance, the loving epithet 'birdie' is translated from the German word *Vöglein*, meaning a little bird. It is interesting to conjecture whether this derives from the age-old St. Valentine's Day association of the mating of birds with the mating of lovers. It might well be that our present day slang expression 'a bird', meaning a casual girl friend, derives from this origin.

Whether or not this is a valentine is debatable, for no month is shown. But this omission is negligible, for a written valentine did not require always to be dated the 14th of February. Remembering that one's Valentine was also one's sweetheart, it would be usual to write one's valentine in this style. This very fine letter, although possibly a betrothal letter, can in any case be considered in the same category as a valentine, for it served the same purpose.

A very fine example of a lover's greeting, which quite possibly was intended for a valentine is the specimen illustrated in Plate 20. This, believed to have originated in the neighbourhood of Philadelphia some time about 1760, is cleverly designed in the form of an acrostic, a style which became a popular feature on early valentines.

Written with excellent penmanship and embellished with the writer's initials opposite those of his sweetheart, the *pièce de résistance* is the intricately drawn true-love knot bearing his loving messages along every twist. This veritable labour of love is headed by its carefully written title: "On the Paragon of Excellence."

28. Beautifully engraved valentine in colour sent to an address in Glaziers Alley, London, 1798. The hand-written message within says:
"Since I put in a Pane of Glass
For you my most transparent Lass,
My Heart I find is full of Pains,
And your bright form still there remains.
You are my Diamond and my Dear
I am like Putty when you are near;
Then mould me with that hand of thine
And you must be my Valentine."
Courtesy of Haywood Parrott, Aylesbury.

All hail fair vestal, lovely gift of heaven,
Nourished in prudence and in wisdom given.
Neglect not this small present from a friend,
Esteem commences where fierce passions end.
Transcendent Fair resplendent star approve
His pleading reasons who thus seeks your love,
Accept his proffers, take his heart in care.
Cherish his passion in a modest sphere.
How then will heaven our constancy commend.
Empyreal bounties happy moments send,
Refulgent blisses crown us to our end.

In this way the name of his sweetheart is spelled out by the first letter of each line: ANNE THACHER.

As well as not being practical for the purpose, the 18th-century postal services were in most cases too costly for the ordinary person to send a valentine, and as most letters were usually left at the principal inn or post house to be called for, it follows that love-tokens and valentines could best be left at the chosen one's own door, as secretly and as anonymously as possible. A love-token, in the shape of a cut-out heart made of paper, or some other small trifle of a gift suitably decorated would be left hanging on the door knob, whilst a written valentine would be pushed under the door—a custom common in Britain as well as in America.

Designs and types were left entirely to the ingenuity of the young lover concerned, who, with plenty of time on his hands, literally put his heart into his work to produce a charmingly decorated and prettily composed valentine for his sweetheart. From about the year 1800 onwards the American hand-made valentine developed, to be gradually replaced by the manufactured and printed valentine of the 1840s, and it is from this time that the influence of Pennsylvania fraktur work is so often seen. Elsewhere all sorts of processes were employed. Careful handwriting in copperplate style was usual, along with a few flourishes of scroll-work by way

29. Published in colour by John Fairburn, London, in 1797. Of especial interest is the early attempt at lace paper work—the little ovals each containing a flower spray are perforated on the paper. Courtesy of Castle Museum, York.

of decoration, embellished with some water colouring. A popular design was always the True-Lover's Knot, with its several love messages twisting around every loop, so that it took care and time to read. Cut-out work of every description was very general, a piece of paper being folded three times in the shape of a triangle, and then, using a suitable design of hearts, or flowers, or birds, would be cut along one single folded edge, so that when unfolded, the design would then be repeated according to the number of folds. Minute handwriting would then fill in any available space with tender messages of love or esteem, and sometimes they would be coloured.

A typical example of a True-Love Knot, boldly coloured with red predominating, is the one shown in Plate 25. This reads:

Never ending turning round about And as thou see'st the links and crosses here So hast thy beauty been to me a snare By the influence of true love I find I am bereav'd both of heart & of mind So fairest creature look with pity down and do not on thy faithful servant frown But pardon him who doth thy love desire, and doth delight thy beauty to admire On no other then let thy goodness shine in beams of comfort from a face devine So that my rap-turned soul rais'd by thy smiles may pass to bliss forgetting all its foils This boon I ask o grant it fair one do Deny me not so now I'll bid adieu. This true loves Knot to thee my dear I send An emblem of my love without an end Crossing turning winding in and out Never ending round about . . . etc. etc.

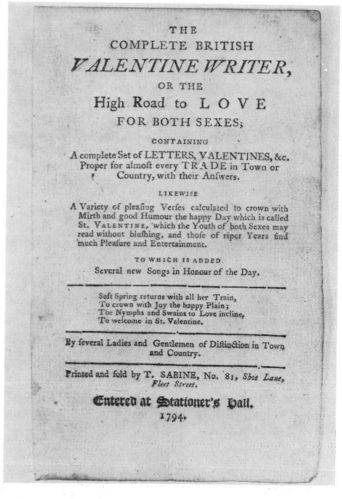

So-called 'puzzle purses' were skilfully made, so that the recipient had always to spend some time trying to decipher the message or verses, and to get the design in the right folds and the right order. A puzzle purse would be square in shape, looking somewhat like a square envelope, which in fact it was. Its four flaps met, folded one inside the other. Each flap was doubled and would sometimes be decorated on both sides. When opened out the whole took on a kaleidoscopic appearance, and the puzzle was not only to read the messages in their right order, but to place the whole contraption back into its right folds.

An excellent example of one of these, which was probably made about 1790, is in the collection of the American Antiquarian Society (Plate 26). Sometimes, a puzzle purse contained a little reward, when, having been unfolded, a lock of hair, or a token of some sort, or maybe a ring, would be revealed.

As with examples of fraktur work, these puzzle purses also originate in Germany, developed from the Irrgarten illuminated manuscripts and prints which were now being printed and made in the districts around Lancaster in Pennsylvania. The German word Irrgarten is best translated to mean labyrinth, and very nearly resembles the popular True-Love Knot, or Endless Knot of Love design which figured so prominently on love letters and love tokens and on valentines. It cannot be definitely stated how True-Love Knots first

originated, but certainly they can be said to date far back; pictures are given of some in an interesting book of curious odds and ends published in 1641. In reading one of these twisting lines it matters not where one starts, for the message meanders on and on.

Among the rarest and much sought after of these early hand-made valentines are those with pin-pricked designs. Pricking out a picture by means of pins was a fashion enjoyed by ladies of leisure in England during the 18th century, as an elegant pastime. The background of a picture, such as furniture, the faces and hands of people and other general details would be painted, and the features and clothing of the persons as well as any fancy border enclosing the picture would be

pricked out by pins of varying thicknesses so as to give an embossed effect, and the whole picture looking very pleasing when finished.

In the British Isles, where similar fashions for love tokens and hand-written valentines also prevailed—although few are known of such early date as American specimens—the first printed valentines were coming into use. The earliest which has so far been noted is dated 1797, although others, hand-made, exist of a much earlier date (Plate 29).

Thus, in this way, the valentine written on paper, was replacing the Valentine as a person, although the custom of drawing for one's Valentine still prevailed, as testified by the frequent references made in the written messages and verses : "You are the same I drew last year. It was because I lov'd you dear." Very often the same phrase or cliché turns up in valentine verses, which points to the popularity of the little books called *Valentine Writers*. The illustration shows an interesting specimen, dated 1794, from the John Johnson Collection in Oxford.

By the turn of the century, in Britain, the old valentine customs were still being strongly maintained although they differed in various parts of the kingdom, and it is interesting to note how, when February was drawing nigh, magazines never failed to observe the event and would print appropriate sonnets and verses to commemorate the 14th of February. The March 1783 issue of *The Hibernian* carries a long poem entitled "The Female Valentine", which twists the use of the word Valentine by suggesting that it is anachronistic for a man to address a female as his Valentine, and recommends that the name Delia be substituted instead for Valentine whenever a man is making the advances!

William Hone, who collected so many unusual traditions and folk-lore customs together,[1] in the British Isles, says that in some places, and more particularly in London, a young man's Valentine is the first maid he sees in the morning, who is not an inmate of the same house, and a girl's Valentine is the first youth she sees.

[1] *Hone's Every Day Book*, 2 vols., 1826; *Hone's Year Book*, 1832.

34. A very fine True-Love Knot, having the Endless Knot of Love in the form of a labyrinth. Hand drawn and coloured, c. 1790-1800. Courtesy of Free Library, Philadelphia.

35. Engraved in sepia by Bartolozzi, c. 1800. On the left, the motif of the Endless Knot of Love, and on the right, the well-known 'Sailor's Farewell'. Author's Collection.

Hone then quotes a few lines from the poet John Gay which mentions this where a rustic housewife reminds her husband:

> I early arose just at the break of day,
> Before the sun had chas'd the stars away;
> A field I went, amid the morning dew
> To milk my kine, (for so should house-wives do,)
> Thee first I spied, and the first swain we see
> In spite of Fortune shall our *true-love* be.

Quoting from the *Connoisseur* of February 20, 1756, Hone describes this same custom in more curious circumstances when certain peculiar ceremonies take place the night before.

Last Friday was Valentine's day, and, the night before, I got five bay-leaves, and pinned four of them to the four corners of my pillow, and the fifth to the middle; and then, if I dreamt of my sweetheart, Betty said we should be married before the year was out. But to make it more sure, I boiled an egg hard, and took out the yolk, and filled it with salt; and when I went to bed, ate it, shell and all, without speaking or drinking after it. We also wrote our lovers' names upon bits of paper, and rolled them up in clay, and put them into water: and the first that rose up was to be our valentine. Would you think it, Mr. Blossom was my man. I lay abed and shut my eyes all the morning, till he came to our house; for I would not have seen another man before him for all the world.

And again we are reminded of Ophelia, who waited at her window to be seen first for a Valentine.

4

REGENCY ELEGANCE

EARLY 19TH-CENTURY VALENTINES–DEVELOPMENT
OF EMBOSSED AND LACE-PAPER WORK
–POST OFFICE CONCERN OVER RUDE VALENTINES
–'VALENTINE WRITERS'–THE REGENCY PERIOD TO 1840

36. Made by Dobbs and postmarked in 1824, this valentine shows a typical Dobbs border, the embossed designs with captions in French. The floral decoration is hand-coloured and the centrepiece is a puzzle purse, which conceals a beautiful flower cage, inside which is a pretty hand-painted picture. Author's Collection.

A FEW years before the turn of the nineteenth century a new fashion in writing paper gradually came about. Writing paper, which hitherto had always been plain, was now being produced with ornamental and fancy edges, and occasionally with printed designs. Examples are known of Italian, Austrian and German origin, and, judging from the few specimens seen, could not have been much in general use, probably due to the cost. The decoration was sometimes floral and usually in colour, but examples are known in two and three colours having the appearance of being stencilled. Specimens in the author's collection date from 1790, and show little costumed figures placed in different positions on double sheets of paper. Other examples show an engraved border printed in green with little winged cupids florally entwined among decoration. It was this type of paper which was to influence the printed valentine sheets which not long afterwards became so very popular. At the time of the French Revolution, the many new French government departments and committees used writing paper lavishly embellished with the new symbols and emblems of the French Republic. Some were only roughly printed, but often they were handsomely engraved. In France, too, writing paper was available to her soldiers and sailors printed or engraved with patriotic motifs showing soldiers bravely posed and warships under sail. In England, where trades people had for long used handsomely engraved letter sheets and bills advertising their trade, and where beautiful printing, often decorative, was used for all manner of everyday requirements, attention turned to the embellishment of writing paper. By 1797 specially printed writing sheets, quarto sized and double paged, were on the market in honour of St. Valentine's Day.

Some of these early valentines were engraved by the well-known Francesco Bartolozzi (1727-1815)—the right-hand example illustrated in Plate 35 being the one most commonly seen. There were many reprints done of this, the same design appearing as late as the 1830s, when it was published hand-coloured, but with Bartolozzi's name removed.

Born in Florence, Bartolozzi studied art in Rome and later became eminent for his fine engraving. He developed his own particular style known as stipple, distinguished by the use of varying shades and sizes of dots, instead of the usual method of line. Coming to England in 1764, he was eventually appointed Engraver to the King.

Although hand-made valentines and True-Lovers' Knots were commonly used during the 18th century in Britain, examples today are hard to find, and most likely they have long since crossed the Atlantic to enhance the many fine collections of valentines in America. Fine engraving had for long excelled in Britain, and now valentines beautifully engraved or with embossed decoration very quickly became popular. The fine example shown in Plate 32 is dated 1802 and is interesting because it also shows an early attempt at lace work, an art which was eventually to make English-made valentines pre-eminent of their kind.

It is not known when paper lace making first started, but it is known that a form of lace work consisting of perforated holes of different sizes on paper was introduced into England from France early in the nineteenth century (*see* Appendix III).

The firm of Dobbs, known to have commenced business as fancy paper manufacturers and stationers in 1803 under the name of H. Dobbs and Co. of 8 New Bridge Street, London, became well known for its very fine and superbly decorated and embossed paper. A great number of early English valentines bear the imprint of this firm, and because the firm changed its name every time a new partner joined, or a new business association was formed, collectors can find great interest in seeking the different names in the various issues and sets of valentines brought out by them. The earliest and scarcest of these bear the name 'DOBBS PATENT' and 'DOBBS', to be followed by 'DOBBS & CO.' All of these were in use up to the 1830s, but those with 'DOBBS' most likely appeared after 1810. Again, after 1838 the imprint was changed to 'H. DOBBS & CO.',

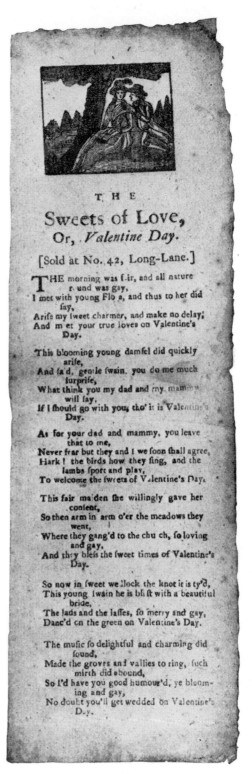

37. A penny sheet of a sort sold in the streets, 1820. Courtesy of John Johnson Collection, Oxford.

38. A collection of Valentine verses published by the Catnach Press, Seven Dials, 1833. This sort of cheap printing sold for one penny. Courtesy of John Johnson Collection, Oxford.

then in 1845-46, to 'DOBBS BAILEY & CO.' Finally, after 1851, their valentines are identified by the name 'DOBBS, KIDD & CO.' The names are as a rule to be found embossed in very small lettering in a central position beneath the design or near to the border. Having a coloured edge and being exquisitely embossed, Dobbs' paper is easily recognisable. Sometimes there was no central ornament or decoration which allowed for a design or a message to be written by hand, but usually the paper was embellished with a hand-coloured floral motif, and quite often the little amorous sentiments embossed around the edges and in each corner were given in French.

Embossing on cards and paper had already reached a high standard of perfection in England by 1796, when the first English patent for the embossing of paper was granted to John Gregory Hancock; excellent work towards the end of the 18th century was likewise being done in Germany, the names of A. Muthenthaler and T. Lang having been noticed. The embossing was produced by placing the paper upon an engraved die and then subjecting it to pressure. Among English embossers of note must be mentioned Charles Whiting, of Beaufort House, Strand, London, who from the 1820s onwards carried on a business engraving and embossing all sorts of cards, tickets and bills. Charles Whiting was one of the few who received an award for a postage stamp design offered by the Treasury in 1839, when a plan for a uniform Penny Postage was under discussion. In America, the earliest known embosser was Samuel N. Dickenson of 52 Washington Street, Boston, who embossed cards for writing and for invitations, etc.

Credit for the art of lace paper making is attributed to Joseph Addenbrooke who had worked with the firm of Dobbs. Before 1840, paper to be embossed was laid on a die and then hammered out with a lead hammer. By chance in 1834 Addenbrooke stumbled on the idea of filing off the raised part of the paper which was laid on the die, thereby creating a lacy effect. He subsequently set up in business manufacturing lace paper on his own at 101 Hatton Garden, in London, and became well known for the high quality of his work. Lace-paper work was eventually done by a number of firms and English made paper of this sort came to be acknowledged as the finest in the world.

Generally speaking, the majority of valentines made in the years before 1840 were not only pretty, but

39. A hand-made valentine, dated 1803; the centre-piece is a stipple engraving and hand-coloured, which is a distinct asset to an otherwise rather amateur piece of cut-out work. Courtesy of A. R. Alcock, Cheltenham.

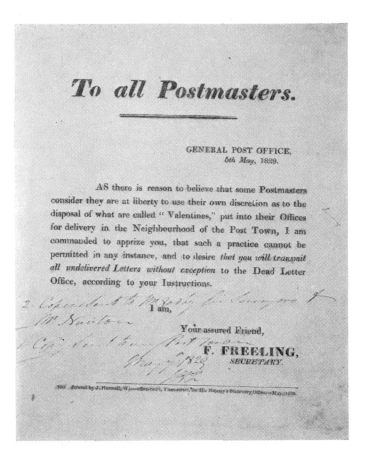

To all Postmasters.

GENERAL POST OFFICE,
5th May, 1829.

AS there is reason to believe that some Postmasters consider they are at liberty to use their own discretion as to the disposal of what are called " Valentines," put into their Offices for delivery in the Neighbourhood of the Post Town, I am commanded to apprize you, that such a practice cannot be permitted in any instance, and to desire *that you will transmit all undelivered Letters without exception* to the Dead Letter Office, according to your Instructions.

I am,

Your assured Friend,

F. FREELING,
SECRETARY.

40. G.P.O. notice of 1829. Rude and unwanted valentines presented a problem to the Post Office when the recipient, who had paid the postage upon delivery, demanded a refund on finding an insulting valentine, sent anonymously. Courtesy of H.M. Postmaster-General.

beautiful, and the sentiments which they carried, either written by hand or printed, were invariably nauseatingly sentimental in style. But not all were pleasant, for letters preserved in the Records Room of the London General Post Office tell of irate fathers called upon to pay postage for insulting and rude valentines sent to their plain daughters, and of people complaining of rude letters sent to them on St. Valentine's Day. The Post Office was now being commonly used for the sending of valentines, for, by the turn of the century, several cities and towns throughout the kingdom, as well as London, enjoyed the facilities of a local Penny Post, which allowed for a letter to be carried over a prescribed radius around and about the city or town for the price of one penny. By 1815 practically every city and town, also a large number of smaller places and villages, was served by its own Penny Post[1] so that valentines could be easily and cheaply carried by this method. Payment, however,

was usually made upon delivery, so that on St. Valentine's Day it sometimes happened that certain people maliciously posted valentines of an obnoxious nature to persons against whom they had a spite or a grudge, or merely to be objectionable. These valentines were sent anonymously, as was the custom, and having to pay postage upon them was actually adding insult to injury. The annoyance caused to those receiving such abusive valentines can well be imagined. Complaints were sent to the local postmasters with a request for the refund of the money expended on such a frivolous and wasted postage. After being referred to higher authority, a ruling was made in March 1817 by the Solicitor to the Post Office:

Valentine Letters

I doubt the propriety of returning the postage for Valentine Letters.

Numerous persons are anxious to receive them and after seeing or reading the Contents, are as anxious to have their Money back.

It is of some importance as to Revenue and I do not think the parties have a fair claim to a return of postage; they should be cautious of taking in Letters at this particular Season.

A. Perkin.
28 March 1817.

The practice becoming more and more general caused Sir Francis Freeling, Secretary of the Post Office, to report on the matter to the Postmaster-General. On February 16, 1824, he wrote:

I am induced to bring the subject of the postages charged on *Valentines*, sent by Post, before your Lordship, more especially as I have this day 8 or 10 applications from the Country, claiming a return of such postage.

I must premise that from time immemorial the Post Office has *not* refunded postage on any thing of that description, but that in the year 1817 I made it a distinct question to the Law Officer of the Department, his opinion which, I now enclose, is clear and to the point, and has hitherto justified the old and immemorial practice of not returning the postage.

We have however invariably relieved the applicants when there was any thing gross or personally offensive

[1] In London, by the Twopenny Post, which in 1801 had taken the place of the London Penny Post.

41. Drawn by Lewis Marks, published 1825. Comic valentines as early as this date are rare. Courtesy of John Johnson Collection, Oxford.

42. Comic valentine, c. 1830–40, published by Torond of Soho London. Courtesy of St. Bride Printing Library, London.

in the communication, and I have even proceeded further by ordering the postage to be reduced to a single letter when the Valentine has been sent in an Envelope.

Your Lordship is well aware that we are in the habit of using a discretionary power in cases of applications to be relieved from the payment of postage on Letters *evidently unnecessary*, viz. such as are sent for the wanton purpose of putting the parties to expense, anonymous letters, not relating to the occupation of the person to whom addressed, letters of a scurrilous and threatening nature, etc., etc. The Solicitor in his opinion as to these Valentines was aware of the exercise of that discretion and he draws the line distinctly. I am led now to place this matter before your Lordship because the number of applications already made is unusually great, and it is evident to common observation that the public considers Revenue-Laws and regulations less binding . . . than it formerly did. Your Lordship after perusing the Solicitor's opinion, will have the opportunity of deciding whether this construction and view of the case are sound and not to be departed from, with the exception of that discretion which I have already adverted to . . .

To this, the Postmaster-General, Lord Chichester, replied that he agreed entirely with the Solicitor.

But the Post Office continued to be bothered, and three years later on February 17, 1827, Freeling again wrote to the Postmaster-General, quoting instances where he thought fit to refund the postage. He says:

In further elucidation of this subject I enclose 2 applications I have received this morning: the one from Mr. Robinson of Huddersfield claiming a return of the postage on 2 Valentines Letters addressed to his Daughters. There is nothing immoral or offensive in these Letters; they appear to be in the usual strain of such productions at this season of the year, and may be fairly called legitimate Valentines, on these we should *not* return the postage.

The other application from the Reverend Edward Kempe is different, this is an Enclosure and an Envelope, and on this we should return *one* rate even if the enclosed were a fair Valentine, but as it is a vulgar Engraving, with insulting lines under written we should consider this a case for a return of the whole postage . . .

If you should to your Friends impart,
The soft effusions of my Heart,

Nor are they like to take't amiss. If Lovers will them with a Kiss.

That maids delight in Billet Doux.

Communication never shews.

O may they give the kind advice,
To make me happy in a trice.

43. This charming valentine in Regency design carries a postmark of the 1830s. Author's Collection.

Quite apart from these reported instances, these old Post Office records reveal such a human understanding existing between a government official and a member of the public and show how conscientiously its officers employed themselves in the discharge of their duties—even those in such a high and exalted position as Sir Francis Freeling, who was undoubtedly the most important person in the whole Post Office administration. He would concern himself with a personal complaint of this nature, and when necessary would refer a matter to the Postmaster-General as to whether this person or that should have a postage refunded! The very personal connection here between the Post Office and the public is very noticeable.

The reference which he makes to envelopes is interesting because they were not generally used at this time, and an enclosure within an envelope counted as a double rate of postage, for postage rates were assessed according to the number of sheets or pieces of paper, as well as the distance over which the letter was to be carried, and the use of an envelope would automatically incur a double postage. So that valentines—and in these years they were invariably quarto sized and double paged, rating thereby as a single sheet of paper—would be folded into the size and shape of an ordinary envelope, sealed with wax and then given into the Post Office.

The 14th of February was a day looked forward to by many a maid, young or old, for this was the day of days when a lover could prove his affection for his beloved by sending her adequate testimony in the shape of a valentine, and when an unknown admirer might appear whose attentions had hitherto not been noticed. For the timid male, too, uncertain whether his approaches were welcome, the opportunity was given to proclaim himself, and if he hadn't the ability to compose his own sentimental verses or pen his amorous message suitably, there were plenty of *Valentine Writers* on sale to help him. These little books were published frequently, and judging from the numbers of varying names and different publishers, must have been in great demand. They cost very little, the common ones being only one penny, and superior ones selling for sixpence.

The same sort of thing was on sale in America too. These little books catered for every sort of taste, from the heavy sentimental, the comic, down to the lewd. They provided suitable verses for every kind of person; for those in the army or navy, both for officers and for

44. A woodcut, English, c. 1820, in red, green and blue. Courtesy of W. Bonwitt, London.

men; for those in trade or profession; for those away from home, for the love-lorn and lonely, for young and old; suitable lines were offered to fit every occasion, and appropriate answers were provided as well to send in reply to what had been received.

In the *Polite Valentine Writer; or, LOVE'S CHAPLET*, published in London about 1810, the following is proposed:

Valentine to a Widow

A widower to a widow sues,
And hopes his suit she'll not refuse,
You have a child and so have I,
They may cement affection's tie.

1835.]	FEBRUARY.	7

Birds, this month, do bill and coo;
Do the like, and you may rue.
Courting is a pretty pleasure;
Wed in haste, repent at leisure.
. . . .
To hen-peck'd husbands what a feast!
This month, all women talk the least.

M D	Season's Signs.	Odd Matters.	WEATHER.
		VALENTINE'S DAY.	Rain or hail,
1	mizzle	I can't make out what they're about,	☽ ♉
2	drizzle	Nor how the men incline;	
3	frizzle	I've watch'd each knock, since nine o'clock,	snow or sleet
4	raw	To get a Valentine.	☉ ♊ ♓ ♓
5	thaw	In vain I've tried, on every side,	in
6	hearts	Some happy chance to see,	this month
7	darts	For, ah, alas! there comes to pass	☌ ♈ ♒ ♄ ✳
8	smarts	No Valentine for me.	you're
9	loves	From morn till night I've scream'd " The light	sure to meet.
10	doves	Guitar," above a week,	' ♀ ☋ ☿
11	gloves	" Bid me discourse" has made me hoarse,	If you don't
12	willing	Till I can scarcely speak.	♊ ☌ ⊕ ♓
13	billing	Through rain and snow I always go	why then
14	wooing	To Tuesday evening lecture,	you won't:
15	cooing	Yet snow and rain don't bring a swain;	♉ ♅ ♑ ♎ ✳
16	eyes	And why, I can't conjecture.	Perhaps
17	sighs	In short, to find a lover kind,	there won't
18	mate	I've us'd all honest ways,	be one
19	fate	I've pinch'd my toes, and no one knows	
20	love	How tight I've lac'd my stays.	
21	cold	Three times to-day, across the way,	♃ ☉ ♐ ♋ ♉
22	scratch	The postman has been seen—	nor t'other:
23	scold	And this makes four,—at Jones's door!	♋ ☿
24	fight	One! two! " For Betty Green."	Why then
25	bite	Well! on my word, old Major Bird	'twill happen
26	spite	Stands making signs, I think,—	♊ ☿ ✳
27	mope	(If Betty dares to set her snares,—)	in
28	rope	I'm sure I saw him wink.	some other.
		I vow I'll call, and tell it all;	
		They'll give her instant warning;	
		And, but the river makes one shiver,	
		I'd drown to-morrow morning.	

Our fortunes I believe are equal,
Let's join to make a pleasing sequel,
At least such is my fond design,
If you'll consent, dear Valentine.

To this an answer in refusal is suggested :

Resolved no more to be a wife,
But e'en to lead a widow's life;
I must the amorous suit decline,
Which you have made, my Valentine,
I pray you do not take offence,
I own you have both worth and sense;
Had second wedlock been my plan,
'Tis you alone would be the man.

And, alternatively, a favourable reply :

Good sir, I like the plan you've sent,
And thank you for the compliment;
In harmony we will combine,
To cherish both your child and mine,
If others should our marriage bless,
It may increase our happiness;
I shall expect you, sir, at four,
That we may talk this matter o'er,
And on our wedding day agree,
As we regale on toast and tea.

FEBRUARY.

45. From *Tom Hood's Comic Annual*, 1835.

For those a little advanced in years was offered:

My cottage is plac'd by a murmuring rill,
Which gently glides at the foot of the hill;
My garden's well stock'd, my cellars are stor'd,
And plentiful neatness is seen at the board.

My dealings in trade was with competence crown'd,
I retir'd at fifty, with many a pound
By industry got—and with honesty mine;
Will you share it with me, my fair Valentine?

For wearied I am of a bachelor's life,
And want that great blessing, a good natured wife;
Our ages are equal, and I hope you'll agree,
Unto the proposals, that I've made to thee.

A proposal of this sort was considered too good a one evidently to turn down, for no refusal is suggested. But the acceptance offered says:

Your Valentine has me delighted,
To find myself no longer slighted;
At fifty I was indeed afraid,
That I should exit an old maid,
This is the truth, dear Valentine,
So now you know my heart is thine.

When the rat-tat of the postman was heard along the street on St. Valentine's Day, many a front room curtain was drawn aside, for the post was anxiously awaited. To be passed by was a fearful experience, and besides, was observed by the next-door neighbour, who was doing the same thing. Tom Hood has given us a lively sketch of a street scene on St. Valentine's Day, but a more subdued and realistic picture is shown in Plate 45.

Where the Post Office was concerned, the 14th of February was one of the busiest days of the year, only exceeded by Election time, when preparations were required to be made to cope with the extra work involved. We are told how the authorities, ever mindful of keeping down expenses, rewarded the Letter Carriers (as postmen were called in those days) with "the usual very moderate sum" for the extra work they were called upon to do. Writing to the Postmaster-General on February 11th, 1835, Sir Francis Freeling said:

It may be necessary to mention that on or about St. Valentine's Day, there is a most extraordinary influx of many thousand letters—to the Twopenny post in particular . . . even former years we have had an addition

46. A puzzle purse, German, c. 1780–90. When unfolded and opened up, a flower-cage is revealed which conceals a tenderly written verse in German, printed on pink silk. Courtesy of K. Gregory Collection, New York.

47. A beautiful hand-coloured lithograph of the Regency period. Courtesy of Castle Museum, York.

48

50, 51. Two reprints from the original plates by James Kendrew of York, in 1820–1830. The lower was named after Halley's Comet of 1835. Courtesy of The London Museum.

50

49

51

48. "Love and Duty", a cheaply printed valentine of the 1830–40s. Author's collection.

49.   "Tho' thou art far away across the sea
        To thee this token of affection I consign
        And may'st thou soon return to me
        And be my ever constant Valentine."

Published by Richardson & Son, Derby. Courtesy of A. R. Alcock, Cheltenham.

52. A very rare letter sheet, "Le Galant Militaire", published in Calais about 1820. Courtesy of Norcross Collection, New York.

of 50, or 60,000 Letters, consequently every possible exertion is necessary on our part to prevent delay and interruption to the general Mass of correspondence.

We summon every hand and every effort is applied to that object, the difficulties are therefore less than they previously would be. I have prepared Mr. Smith (Superintending President of the Twopenny Post Office) accordingly, and we shall at least do as well this year as we have hitherto done.

I shall have to submit hereafter that the usual very moderate sum be allowed to the Letter Carriers for refreshments, etc. to get through the extraordinary exertions of the 2 or 3 days . . .[1]

When Tom Hood drew his picture, Britain was enjoying a period when grace and elegance prevailed everywhere, for this followed the Regency period and it was admirably reflected in the designs of valentines. Boldly drawn, yet simple in design, they show a charm of their own and a beauty quite different from those of the Victorian era, which was about to be ushered in.

[1] P.M.G.'s Report No. 77 of 1835.

A popular motif of this period, one which is keenly sought after by collectors today, was the so-called 'flower-cage' design (sometimes called 'cobweb' or 'bee-hive'). This novelty, like so many others, probably originated in Germany, as is shown by the early specimen illustrated in Plate 46, which dates to about the late 18th century. Skilful cutting out of threads of paper either circular or square-shaped which could be lifted by a small piece of cotton in the centre, produced a bee-hive effect when raised; underneath would be a small picture, or a lovingly written verse, and sometimes a lock of hair. This cut-out paper work was so frequently done over a floral design, such as a rose or a cluster of flowers that, appropriately the name 'flower cage' was given. The name 'bee-hive' also applied because similar novelties in the way of surprises, views of well-known places and comic pictures, which were in no way connected with valentines, had been popular since the turn of the century, and were known as bee-hives. Today specimens of this sort are commonly referred to as 'cobweb'.

53. Bundle Valentine. Printed in brown on silk, c. 1800. Courtesy of Norcross Collection, New York.

The flower-cage valentine shown in Plate 57 is a good example. Beautifully printed and hand coloured on paper made by Dobbs, two peaches are depicted instead of flowers. These have been cleverly cut to allow for the whole of the central part to be lifted. Sometimes a design contained a double 'cobweb', usually two blossoms side by side, which is very rare to find; an exceptional specimen in the K. Gregory collection in New York shows as many as four 'cobwebs' on the one valentine. These flower-cage valentines were sometimes made by hand, when the paper threads forming the 'cobweb' would be cut a little wider, and very ingenious surprises would be arranged carefully hidden underneath to delight the eye of whoever was intended to lift the thread. The painstaking work required in making one of these can well be imagined, and they were often combined with hand-written verses.

Prominent, too, at this time were valentines showing sailors. They are usually depicted when taking farewell of, or returning to, their sweethearts, with inevitably a bundle over the shoulder. This bundle was sometimes in itself a form of valentine, and both the Norcross and the Hallmark collections in America have fine examples of these.

The bundle valentine illustrated in Plate 53 is printed in brown on silk and is about 30 inches square. This piece of material, suitably worded with loving expressions of endearment, would be brought back by a sailor as a gift to his sweetheart, who used it as a reticule for carrying odds and ends, or as a headscarf. But sometimes the girl friend made a gift of a 'bundle' to her sailor boy, when it would be made of stronger material and somewhat larger, so that he could bundle his belongings in it and carry it over his shoulder. Probably originating in Salem, Massachusetts, in the 1800s, they are a part of American tradition. Such souvenirs are extremely scarce today, but the silk kerchief sort, as given to the girl, was greatly treasured, and some have been carefully preserved in sea-faring families in America.

Bearing in mind that the first fifteen years of the century were unsettled ones, with Britain at war with the French, it was natural for valentines to be published showing the parting of soldiers and sailors from their loved ones, and for some to have a patriotic theme. Some of these were woodcuts cheaply printed and garishly tinted, but mostly they were finely lithographed and pleasantly coloured; proof of their popularity is

54. A sailor with his bundle – coloured woodblock, c. 1840. Author's Collection.

55. A beautiful "flower-cage" on paper embossed by Westwood. Early 1840s. Author's Collection.

56. A Theorem, or Poonah valentine—about 1845. American. Reproduced by courtesy of Norcross Collection, New York.

their long life, for they continued far into the Victorian era. An interesting one shows a man-o'-war. This was made having a side of the ship that opened to reveal a sailor, attended by Cupid, writing to his loved one; in a similar example the whole stern of the ship opens. The well-known valentine collector, Jonathan King the younger, commented on this particular valentine in his notes, and explained that the artist was a man named Ross, who went and drowned himself because he fancied that his invention of the opening sides had passed unnoticed, yet he thought his idea so wonderful.

Some years later another form of this novelty was published having the design of a church, with a door that opened, disclosing a wedding taking place. These kinds of valentines are very rare.

For the most part, valentines of the Regency years were delightfully designed, usually lithographed with a simplicity of line and charmingly coloured. In these years the artist George Corbould designed several delightful valentines, and Alfred Crowquill, too, produced a great many in his inimitable style (*see* Plate 59). Other artists of note of this period were Nelson, Bourier, J. H Jones, Clayton, Richardson and Sheldrake. The cheaper valentines sold for sixpence, and the better ones for one shilling and sixpence.

Some valentines were printed in copperplate, and a series made by James Kendrew of York in 1820 was later reprinted when the plates came into the possession of Andrew Tuer of the Leadenhall Press. Tuer had thirteen of these plates which, many years later, he reprinted for Jonathan King (*see* Appendix IV) to sell to collectors. They were sold only as reprints and some of them

Can one poor humble verses my fair
Of love the power and truth declare ?
Can genius joind with words impart

The warm affection Of the heart
Ah! no - since all my love must be
But known by deeds of love for Thee

57. A 'flower-cage' or 'cobweb' valentine on embossed paper by Dobbs, postmarked in the 1820s. By lifting a thread, the two peaches are raised to reveal a small heart inscribed with a message of love. Author's Collection.

58. Circa 1840. The side of the ship opens to show Cupid giving inspiration to a sailor, who is writing to his sweetheart. Courtesy of St. Bride Printing Library, London.

he coloured. Originals are very rare, and one is in the Hallmark collection. Jonathan King tried to buy the plates from the Tuer estate, but never succeeded. One plate, the famous one known as Halley's Comet, is in the K. Gregory collection, and another showing a couple on a bench is in the Hallmark collection; a third is privately owned in London.

Andrew Tuer is remembered for his book on the life of the engraver Bartolozzi. He was a printer and publisher and an authority on children's books. He was also a keen collector with many interests and acquired a very fine collection of valentines; two of his albums are now in the John Johnson collection at Oxford.

Although at this time, vulgar and comic valentines were still generally used (as proved by the complaints sent to the General Post Office), very few of these are to be found today, and they are certainly scarce, although those of a later date published during the Victorian era

are commonly to be found. Some of these early comic valentines were drawn by the Cruikshank brothers, George and Robert; a fine example is the one shown in Plate 60 by Robert Cruikshank. In his young days, George Cruikshank designed school pieces, which were specially printed sheets for school children to show their cleverness and dexterity in handwriting. It is said that his employer more than once shut him in an empty room, with a bottle of gin for company, which he wasn't allowed to leave until he had finished his work!

Abroad, commonly in Austria and Germany, the Lovers' Greetings Cards known as Freundschaftskarten were being produced in abundance, and were often of exquisite beauty. Occasionally they took the form of an embossed design with a printed message on coloured silk beneath a small flap. Often they were delicately printed, and sometimes a movable tag changed a picture or produced a concealed message. Some of the prettiest of these were published in Vienna and Prague. But the most beautiful of all were Viennese, made out of coloured tinsel and gauze with finely made little scraps of floral decoration surrounding a little picture amorously designed and containing a simple loving message. An artist of repute who designed some of the prettiest of these Viennese cards was Johann Endletzbergen (1799-1856). His cards are readily identified by the initials J. E. in very small print at the foot.

In France, too, very elegant greetings cards, known as *cartes d'amitiés* and containing tender messages, were on the market. They were often beautifully printed on embossed or lacy paper, or sometimes ornamentally printed on note-paper, with envelopes to match. They mostly belong to the 1840s, and although not dedicated to St. Valentine's Day their use was probably stimulated by the prevailing fashion and popularity for valentines in England.

In America, during the early part of the century, valentines were customarily made by hand, and despite the Puritan attitude of a few places in the New England States, where sentimental missives of this sort were not always encouraged and were liable to be frowned on, beautiful and lovingly made work in the shape of love letters, True-Love Knots and puzzle purses was done, with the influence of the Pennsylvania German fraktur style sometimes apparent.

Another form of home-made valentine was made by drawing or tracing all the outlines and the designs on oil

59. Two Comic Valentines drawn respectively by Alfred Crowquill (1841) and Robert Cruickshank, who was fond of giving
animal faces to his characters, (1825). Courtesy of John
Johnson Collection, Oxford

paper. A stencil was then cut and after colouring with
ordinary water colour, the design was fixed by brushing
over with a solution of gum arabic. Usually the picture
took the form of a flower, the process lending itself
more easily to this sort of design, but anything fanciful
and colourful and easy to stencil was chosen. This kind
of work is called 'Theorem' or 'Poonah' work, having
originated in India (*see* Plate 56).

60. English, c. 1820. Cupid presenting the Chart of Love that
the Sailor may know where to find his Sweetheart; hand-
coloured lithograph.

'THE GOLDEN ERA'

INTRODUCTION OF ENVELOPES—EARLY AMERICAN
PUBLISHERS—INTRODUCTION OF ORNAMENT
ON VALENTINE DESIGN—BEGINNING OF
'THE GOLDEN ERA'—FAMOUS VALENTINE MANUFACTURERS

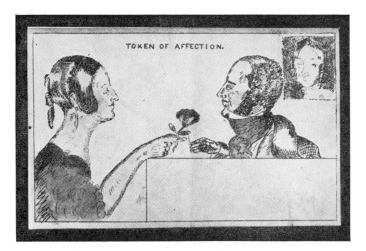

61. Back and front of a rare valentine envelope, one of a series published by **R. W. Hume of Leith. Author's Collection.**

JUST three years after the young Queen Victoria came to the throne, on January 10, 1840, an event of momentous importance took place, which completely changed the writing habits of everyone for all time. This was the introduction of a uniform Penny Post, brought about through the efforts of Rowland Hill and other notable citizens working in collaboration with him.[1] For the price of one penny, a letter weighing half an ounce could now be sent anywhere within the United Kingdom. People who had seldom written before because of the expense, were now able to do so. Relatives were now able to keep in touch, and families could more easily get word from those away from home. The public were made familiar with the new-fangled envelopes, sometimes referred to as 'paper pockets', and an occasion such as St. Valentine's Day was celebrated as never before.

Although the popular size for valentines remained the usual quarto, or letter sheet size—which by common custom would be folded into ordinary envelope size and then fastened by means of sealing wax—the new fashion in envelopes allowed for smaller sheets of paper, and printers and publishers, quick to see the advantages, produced specially printed and decorated envelopes, with matching note paper. These were made available for every sort of occasion, and inevitably suitably designed note-paper and envelopes were made for St. Valentine's Day.

Many of these little envelopes were charmingly decorated, often delicately printed, sometimes embossed, and extremely beautiful. After having served their purpose, they were usually thrown away; whereas

[1] *See* the author's *The Penny Post* (Lutterworth Press, 1964).

the enclosure, which often matched the envelope, would be cherished and put away to be preserved along with other romantic mementoes (the Victorians were fond of keeping such things). This explains why today, collectors like to have both envelope and enclosure, and why there are some who collect only the decorated and pictorial envelopes. A rare example of a valentine envelope is the one shown in Plate 61. Published by Hume of Leith, it forms one of a series, but very few have been recorded. It is the earliest known example of a specially printed envelope for St. Valentine's Day. By far the most usual sort of envelope for special occasions, especially on the 14th of February, was elaborately embossed, and commonly used from the 1840s right through to the 1870s, and even later. Often envelopes were sold matching the valentines, but others were sold in packets for general use. Of interest, too, are the little wafers which were used for sealing the envelope as an alternative to wax. For, at this time, envelopes were manufactured without gum, and could be opened flat. In order to fasten an envelope each of its four flaps had to be sealed. For St. Valentine's Day, prettily designed wafers, often in colour and with a suitable motto, were available for this purpose. Even after 1845, when envelopes were beginning to be on the market with gummed flaps, the use of these little paper wafers was general.

As a consequence of the propaganda carried on in Great Britain for a cheap postage, which resulted in a uniform penny post being established in January 1840, similar agitation took place in some parts of America, principally in New York and Boston. Conditions in America were so vastly different, however, with distances between towns so great, populations much smaller, and places often sparsely populated, that a postal reform of this magnitude was quite impracticable and could not be considered by the American Post Office. It was therefore left to the initiative of private enterprise that, due to loopholes in the American postal laws, local 'Penny Posts' were established in many towns throughout America. The first was The New York Penny Post, which came into being in the early part of January 1840. For the price of three cents, a letter was collected and delivered within certain limits of the city. Other local, or Penny Posts, were not long in opening up in other towns and cities throughout the country, the postage varying as a rule from one cent to three cents for a letter. For, in America, the term 'a penny' implied (as it

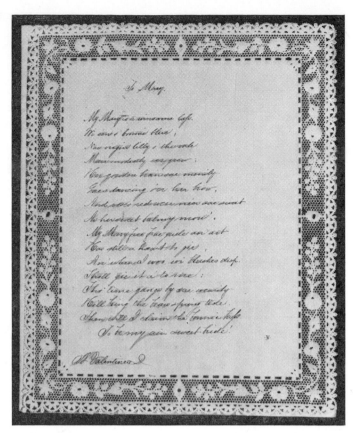

62. It was very usual to write one's own valentine on decorated paper, such as this beautiful little specimen of lace paper. An American valentine of the 1840s, posted in New York through Boyd's City Express Post. Author's Collection.

63. An American valentine envelope, c. late 1840s, carried by Blood's Private Post of Philadelphia. Note the two hearts pierced by an arrow on the flap. Author's Collection.

still does today) a small amount. This meant that on St. Valentine's Day, valentines could be sent easily and cheaply by post for local delivery, and explains why so many American valentine envelopes dated in the early years of the 1840s bear the imprint and postage of one of these private posts. Some of these local stamps add considerable value to a valentine or its envelope, and are much sought after.

In 1845, the United States Post Office introduced cheaper postage, when, for five cents, a letter could be carried a distance of 300 miles. At this time, adhesive postage stamps had not been adopted by the United States Post Office (although some of the private posts used them), so that valentine letters of this period are to be found marked with a '5', sometimes hand-stamped in ornamental design, which of course greatly enhances

the appearance of the envelope or cover and gives extra pleasure to a collector. When posted locally to an address within the town's limits, valentines were stamped with a '2'. Sometimes the special valentine envelope would be a very large one, and the hand-stamped '2' could be extremely small, giving a very odd effect. This two-cent rate is known as the 'drop-letter' rate for a letter posted and collected at the same post office; as there was no delivery it was usual for people to call at the post office for their mail, although private carriers provided a letter delivery, if paid for, when special stamps either adhesive or handstamped, would denote payment. Many of these are extremely rare and greatly enhance the value of a valentine.

From the 1840s the business of making valentines and fancy stationery was a flourishing one, and many pub-

65, 66. American coloured lithograph on Mansell paper, together with its envelope – 1850s. Author's Collection.

67. American envelope, printed in blue with gold linings. Note the little wafer seal on the top of the flap; its message, above and below a wedding ring, says: "Sorrows I divide—Joys I double", c. 1850. Author's Collection.

68. A heavily embossed envelope by Meek, postmarked February 13, 1853. Author's Collection.

65

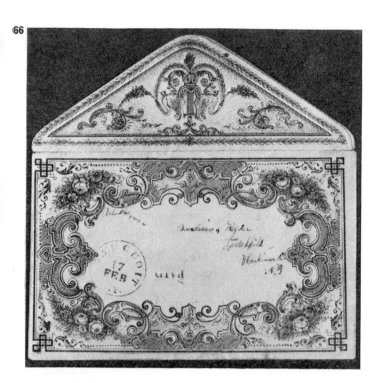

66

68

67

69. An American embossed envelope of the 1000s. Author's Collection.

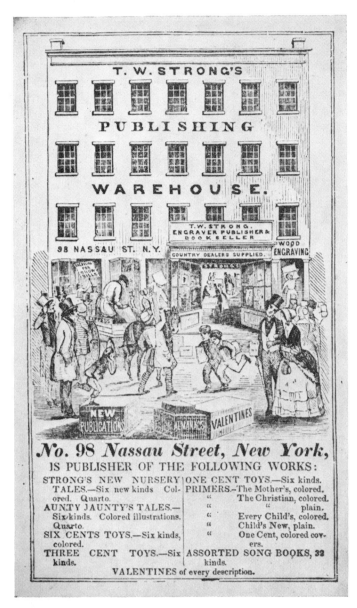

70. T. W. Strong's, 98 Nassau Street, New York: Publishing Warehouse. Courtesy of Carroll Alton Means, Connecticut.

lishers and printers found in it a profitable side-line. It is difficult to trace the names of the many firms involved in this trade owing to the frequency with which they amalgamated or changed their names whilst still carrying on at the same address (*see* Appendix VI). One prominent American firm was Elton & Co., of 98 Nassau Street, New York, which in 1846 claimed to have been the first publisher of valentines in the United States of America. This would set the date to about 1834, when Robert H. Elton, an engraver, commenced business there. Some years afterwards the business was taken over by T. W. Strong, also an engraver, who had been in busi-

ness not far away at 153 Fulton Street. T. W. Strong remained at 98 Nassau Street for several years, publishing valentines, juvenile books and fancy stationery. Later, many comic and vulgar valentines as well were published at this address.

Meanwhile, in England during the 1840s, valentine makers were producing some of their most beautiful work, and it is these valentines of the early Victorian era that appeal so much to the majority of collectors.

The quarto-sized valentine continued to be the size most generally used, thereby allowing more scope for the sort of ornamentation so favoured by the Victorians. Invariably a decorated border surrounded the entire sheet, which sometimes took the form of lace-work or printed fancy work. Often the edges and sides of the paper would be exquisitely embossed, with an almost cameo-like effect for the main motif. In the centre would be a coloured picture, either lithographed or hand coloured, and occasionally embossed overall. Sometimes a small puzzle purse would be placed in the centre which, when unfolded, would reveal the usual expressions of everlasting love and faithfulness, or maybe a little picture romantically drawn. A popular novelty was a metal mirror prettily framed and prominently placed with a suitable couplet or a few words to please whoever looked at it, whilst another favourite was the small daintily printed envelope fixed to the centre of the page, having an appropriately written message inside—the whole piece charmingly decorated.

A particularly pleasing series which is greatly sought after today by collectors in England and in America is often referred to as 'The Unrequited Love' or 'The Despondent Lover' set. On quarto size paper, each valentine of this series is adorned with a lightly embossed decorative border. The central picture of each shows a delightful aquatint, beautifully coloured and finished by hand. Although some of the scenes depict young ladies in grief, and one shows a jilted lover, not all of them are unhappy. In fact, one shows a young lady radiantly pleased with herself clutching a love letter to her bosom; several are insipidly pleasant, whilst one shows a bridal couple leaving a country church surrounded by their friends. The set numbers fourteen in all, which was recognised as the regular 'valentine dozen'. The original publisher of this interesting series, which came out in the 1830s, is believed to be Addenbrooke. It has been noted that a set of this series is known on paper water-

71. A typical woodcut of the cheaper
sort, by A. Park. Author's Collection.

Published by A. PARK, 47, Leonard Street, Finsbury, London.

The pretty doves who bill and coo,
Teach in their fondness how to woo;
Their mutual love, their modest kiss,
Reminds us of connubial bliss!
Who, but themselves, know the delight;
When two fond hearts in love unite,
Soothing each care, in woe or strife,
Which may attend this checquer'd life ;
My faith I pledge thee—plight me thine,
Dearest, be thou my Valentine !

marked '1828', with Addenbrooke's name imprinted. Some time later, it seems likely that the plates came into someone else's possession, who filed off Addenbrooke's name from them and reprinted the entire series on un-watermarked paper. This could explain the plentiful supply still available and the comparatively worn state of the embossing on some copies.

In sharp contrast to these prettily sentimental valentines were the rude and comic ones, which were now being published in great numbers. Today we are inclined to regard the charming and beautiful examples as being typically Victorian, as indeed they are, but equally so are the vulgar ones which depict an aspect and attitude traditionally British, and revealed in many ways other than in this sort of valentine. Indeed, similar dissipated and grotesque characters were often featured in William Hogarth's prints; when looking at some of these comic valentines we are reminded of the unflattering types shown in 'The Harlot's Progress' and 'Gin Lane' and other Hogarth prints of this sort. John Ireland, his friend and biographer, explained that they were "calculated for the lower orders of society". Later in the century Thomas Rowlandson drew much the same sort of characters, as did George Cruikshank some years later. Changing with the times, this sort of vulgar drawing prevailed throughout the whole of Victoria's reign and

72. Early American lithographed valentine. The message, "I'm *off* for California", dates it about 1849. Courtesy of Hallmark Historical Collection.

73, 74. Two notices of Elton & Co., who claimed to have been the first publisher of valentines in the United States of America. Courtesy of Carroll Alton Means, Connecticut.

74

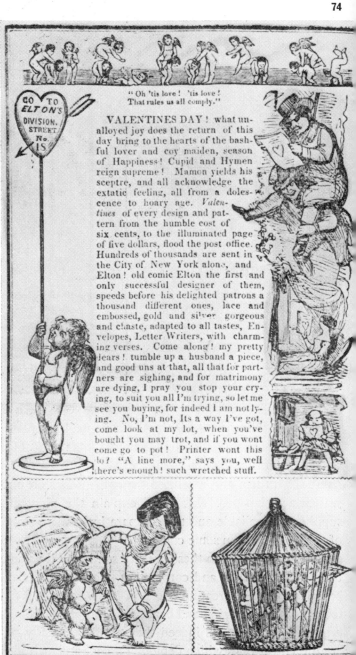

"Oh 'tis love! 'tis love! That rules us all comply."

VALENTINES DAY! what unalloyed joy does the return of this day bring to the hearts of the bashful lover and coy maiden, season of Happiness! Cupid and Hymen reign supreme! Mamon yields his sceptre, and all acknowledge the extatic feeling, all from a dolescence to hoary age. *Valentines* of every design and pattern from the humble cost of six cents, to the illuminated page of five dollars, flood the post office. Hundreds of thousands are sent in the City of New York alone, and Elton! old comic Elton the first and only successful designer of them, speeds before his delighted patrons a thousand different ones, lace and embossed, gold and silver gorgeous and chaste, adapted to all tastes, Envelopes, Letter Writers, with charming verses. Come along! my pretty dears! tumble up a husband a piece, and good uns at that, all that for partners are sighing, and for matrimony are dying, I pray you stop your crying, to suit you all I'm trying, so let me see you buying, for indeed I am not lying. No, I'm not, Its a way I've got, come look at my lot, when you've bought you may trot, and if you wont come go to pot! Printer wont this lot! "A line more," says you, well there's enough! such wretched stuff.

Valentines! Valentines!!

Hear ye! Hear ye! all you forlorn damsels and bashful bachelors, you are hereby notified to repair in due season to

ELTON'S, 98 Nassau-st.

and then and there procure one of his delicious love letters, with their beautiful colored embellishments, and having added a delicate sentiment of your own, seal and direct the same to the dear object of your affections, thereby laying the foundation of the most true of all earthly happiness, viz. matrimony.

ELTON has a few comical Valentines to be sent to fusty old bachelors and sour old maids that are beyond cure. Also, a general assortment of Valentine Writers.

73

75. Circa 1850–60. The postman was often lampooned in valentines. Author's Collection.

76. A clever comic valentine published by Lloyd of Fleet St., c. 1850. This firm was a prodigious publisher of cheap valentines, mostly comic. Author's Collection.

is still enjoyed today, as shown by the so-called comic seaside picture postcards, on which large bosoms and broad posteriors, beer and bottles, red noses and comic faces always appeal to a certain sense of British humour.

Equally typical were the less expensive valentines printed as woodcuts on cheap paper, with the design quickly splashed with colour. Generally a loving couple would be shown hand in hand or singly, the man with an ardent, earnest expression and the maid simpering and coy. The couplets which adorn them sometimes reflect their cheapness, not only by the poor quality of the printing, but also by the verses which would be mis-spelled and almost meaningless.

For example, an elegantly dressed gentleman with walking-stick under his arm is holding the hand of a tight waisted, full-skirted young lady wearing a mob cap, standing in a garden of luxury and extravagance. The verse begins:

> The sun that gilds the gladsom
> The ffowers that dezk the grave
> The berds that fill the trees with mirth,
> All speak to me of love.

77. Typical of the cruel sort of comic valentines published in the 1850s. This example is by P. Huestis of New York. Courtesy of the Norcross Collection, New York.

78. A wonderful example of Mansell's lace work, heavily embossed with cameo-like effect. The metal mirror is surrounded by a gilded wreath, with a little gilt Cupid below. Author's Collection.

The meanest creatures give life,
In someway shows its love:
But faithful love of man and wife,
Is registered in realms above.

Brushed over with streaks of lurid colours, a valentine of this sort was doubtless considered eminently respectable by the person who bought it, and the fact that the wording was incorrectly printed would matter very little, and most likely would not be noticed.

This type of valentine, the vulgar and the comic, as well as the cheaply printed 'respectable' kind, fell far below the high standard of the beautiful specimens which enhance most collections today; nevertheless they should be cherished just as highly, and no collection is complete without examples of this kind. In fact, some are harder to come by because, as a rule, they were used more by the lower classes, and by a section of society unable to keep souvenirs of this type over the years, unlike the more costly items which were put away and treasured for their sentiment and beauty by the more well-to-do and middle class families.

Many of these cheap and comic valentines were reminiscent of the single ballads and penny sheets which were published in great profusion over the years in the district of Seven Dials, St. Giles, London, and particu-

79. Two comic valentines, typical of A. Park's publications. Author's Collection.

80. One of a series of rude valentines designed by John Leighton. Author's Collection.

THE FUNGI.

Hollo! Cupid, now then stupid; what have you got there?
I can't think; so vile a stink does impregnate the air;—
That stink is pride, can't be denied; th'effluvia is so rare—
Salmagundi, crown'd by fungi,—of the mess beware.

He comes of filth, and dirt that's spilth,—a plant of spurious mould—
Form'd in night, a sort of blight, a money muck of gold.
"Fools make money"; tho' 'tis funny, true's the saying old;
"Wise men spend it," comprehend it; I will not be sold.

Nobly kind's the man of mind, he never can be mean;
You, reverse, are proud of purse; aye, every thing unclean;
Arrant fool, you toadies stool,—no Valentine, I ween;
I hope I've sense, I'll take me hence,—with you I'll not be seen.

larly in Monmouth Street, where later, W. S. Fortey took over the famous Catnach Press and published comic valentines in the 1840s. Not far away was another firm, Torond in West Street, Soho. But by far the most prolific of the cheap valentine makers was A. Park of Leonard Street, Finsbury, London, who also produced some splendid hand-coloured lithographs of real beauty. Others were made by J. T. Wood in the Strand, later known as the London Lace Paper and Valentine Company.

Another and more serious firm was Dean & Company, of Threadneedle Street, who issued quantities of comic valentines and were well known for the movable sort where, by pulling a tag, a head wagged or tongue came out, or a leg or an arm moved. These were very popular, although the idea was quite an old one and had long been used for paper toys, and the same thing had been employed on greetings cards in Germany and Austria since the turn of the century. It is said that Deans had a window full of them, with a contrivance that kept them constantly moving. They sold from one penny to sixpence each.

Alfred Henry Forrester, who worked under the name of Alfred Crowquill, was an artist responsible for a number of comic valentines during the 1830s and 1840s. He also contributed to Punch and to The Illustrated London News. Another artist was Wilson, who, according to notes left by Mr. Dean, Jr. of the firm of Dean &

67

81. Advertising sheet of Dean & Co. Courtesy of St. Bride Printing Library, London.

Company, used to design six comic valentines a year.[1] A prominent comic artist who did some clever work during this time under the pseudonym of Luke Limner was John Leighton. His work was decidedly more subtle and his humour more biting and satirical than the usual run of comic valentine artists. He drew some sets of hand-coloured valentines for A. Park of Finsbury about the year 1846, as well as a sarcastic series for Ackermann about 1849 (see Plate 80) and others for Dean & Company early in the 1850s.

Much the same sort of valentines were published in America, where similar tastes prevailed. Along with delightfully printed valentines of the sentimental variety and very pleasing to look at, large numbers of grotesquely printed sheets, rude and comic, were on the market to cater for those who wanted them. Sometimes they had a political angle or featured something topical. Often they were rude and cruel in their humour, and no doubt many were sent anonymously out of spite so as to get even in settling old scores. Many of this kind were printed by the valentine manufacturers; those by Elton, T. W. Strong, and Turner and Fisher are more generally seen today, others by Charles P. Huestis, T. Frere and James Wrigley are more difficult to find. Some were imported from England, along with the more beautiful and sentimental valentines which had always enjoyed a steady sale in the U.S.A.

Another type of valentine which was as popular in America as it was in Britain, was the decorated letter sheet (see Plate 62). Although this would be used on

[1] From a letter written to Andrew Tuer by one of the Dean family.

82

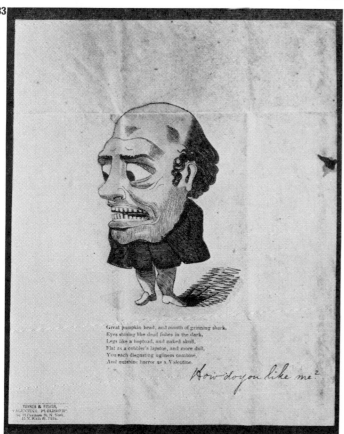

84

82, 83. Two comic valentines published by Turner & Fisher, c. 1850. Courtesy of the Hallmark Historical Collection.

84. A single sheet in the form of a Valentine Writer. Sheets such as these were usually sold in the street for a penny each. Printed by G. Smeeton of 74 Tooley St., London, c. 1820. Courtesy of St. Bride Printing Library, London.

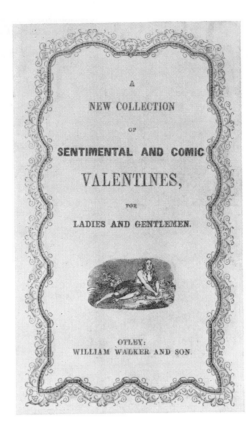

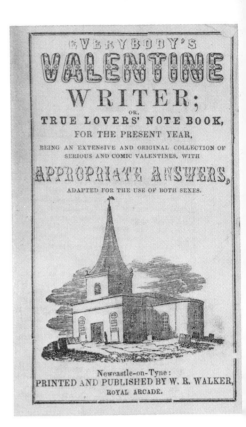

85. *Valentine Writers*, giving a wide variety of valentine verses, were published to suit all tastes.

86. Title page and frontispiece of *The New Comic Valentine Writer*, published by Turner and Fisher, New York & Philadelphia, 1848. Courtesy of Carroll Alton Means, Connecticut.

any occasion, most of those which are seen today are in the form of valentines; their eloquent verses having been written, as a rule, with the aid of a *Valentine Writer*. These little *Valentine Writers* were now being published more than ever before, and suited every need, whether serious or comic. Some people preferred a plain letter sheet with a lacy or embossed border for decoration, enclosing it in an extravagantly embossed envelope, whereas, in America, the fashion generally was for elaborately printed envelopes (*see* Plates 63, 66, 67 and 90).

These years of the 1840s can truthfully be said to represent the golden era of the valentine. The high standard of workmanship which produced such exquisite embossing and such perfect lace paper, together with the beautiful decoration which was applied, makes the collecting of these charming valentines a most delightful pursuit. The valentines made by the long-established firm of Dobbs during these years reflect the high quality which this firm always maintained. Their valentines now showed an abundance of finely made lace paper, having a central ornament or device often backed by fine satin or silk and adorned with daintily coloured

87. An unusually fine example of the circular type of valentine, dating circa 1850. The valentine is formed basically of two lace perforated paper doilies, having the imprint of Meek, and is adorned with real lace and ribbon, together with floral scraps and dried fern wrapped in muslin. Courtesy of A. R. Alcock, Cheltenham.

88. A coloured woodcut, by T. W. Strong, of the late 1840s. Courtesy of Metropolitan Museum of Art, New York (Gift of Mrs. John Sylvester, 1936).

89. A comic valentine published by T. W. Strong, c. 1850. Courtesy of Metropolitan Museum of Art, New York (Gift of Miss Marion W. Emerson, 1948).

floral decoration or perhaps with a few prettily coloured scraps. An innovation started by Dobbs was to have flower petals that could be lifted, showing a little message underneath. These are said to have been made for them by a person named Greer, the arrangement being that he should make for no other firms, and that he should share in the profits.

A rival to Dobbs was Joseph Addenbrooke, who had formerly worked for them and had perfected the art of making lace paper. When he started on his own it is said that he cut their prices by half. The lace paper which he made so nearly resembles real lace, the delicate work often so minute and perfect in detail, that it commands more than a passing glance. His valentines are difficult to find.

Joseph Mansell's work on the other hand is easier to come by, and is equally attractive. He is listed, as early as 1835, in Red Lion Square, in business as a fancy stationer, engraver and printer. In the 1840s his embossing was so perfect that the work can be said to resemble cameos in miniature. Patterned against a delicate surround of paper lace, and sometimes ornamented with small gilded scraps of cupids or with hand-painted clusters of little flowers, with an endearing message neatly written by hand in very small lettering, the finished valentine represented a veritable work of art. Rarest of his valentines are those having a little coloured picture made by the Baxter process; for, sometime about 1849, George Baxter, the inventor of colour printing in oils, sold his patent to a number of licencees of whom Joseph Mansell was one.

It is difficult to name one manufacturer superior to another at this period, for all the leading firms did superb work. As a rule, their names are shown embossed in minute lettering somewhere along the border of the design, or concealed in the ornamentation. Among the better-known makers in the 1840s, whose names appear most frequently, are the following: T. H. Burke of 12 Bull Head Court, Newgate; David Mossman of Islington; George Kershaw and Son, 17 Wilderness Row; George Meek of Crane Court, Fleet Street; W. J. Meek; John Windsor of Clerkenwell and Dean & Company of Threadneedle Street.

About 1845, David Mossman, according to notes given to Andrew Tuer by the son of Mr. Dean, introduced artificial flowers, grouping them tastefully by way of ornament. These valentines were first issued by

90. An American envelope lithographed in bronze, c. 1850s. Similar envelopes were published to take a quarto size valentine, unfolded. Author's Collection.

Ackermann's of the Strand and Regent Street at prices ranging from one to three guineas each, and are said to have been a great success in the West End of London. Afterwards, according to Mr. Dean, this class of flower valentine was manufactured more cheaply and Mossman entered into arrangements with George Kershaw to make them in quantities for the wholesale trade. Considering that the average price for a good class valentine was about 2s. 6d. each, these artificial flower valentines can certainly be considered exceptional.

George Kershaw & Son were one of the largest and most important of the fancy stationers and, apart from their valentines, were well known for their pictorial headed writing paper, showing views of places of interest and beauty of all parts of the kingdom, as well as for their comic seaside note-paper which enjoyed great popularity in the 1850s. Although their quarto-sized valentines of the 1840s are none too common, their

smaller valentines published after the 1850s are often seen. Their standard of workmanship was high and their output prolific. In common with many fancy paper manufacturers, they sold their paper to others to be assembled into valentines. This is an important reason why some collectors prefer those valentines manufactured before the 1850s, when it can generally be assumed that the name showing on the paper is that of the valentine maker. After the 1850s there were a great many people, small shopkeepers and stationers, as well as private individuals who purchased their fancy paper from any of the well-known makers, and made up their own valentines. These sometimes can be easily detected by the mixed decoration used in the assembly. Often two very different sorts of paper would be employed; scraps, not of the same quality as the paper, would be used for ornament and the style would not conform to the overall design. Valentines made by the famous

91

91, 92. A pair of valentines by Kershaw. Valentines of this sort were frequently published in sets or in pairs. Author's Collection.

92

93

94

93. One of the series printed in colour during the 1840s, describing The Marriage Market. Published by Rock & Co., London. Author's Collection.

94. An amusing design in the shape of an advertisement with two pages that lift up. It asks for a companion to assist in domestic arrangements, etc. Adorned with two pink roses on fine lace paper, and exquisitely edged.

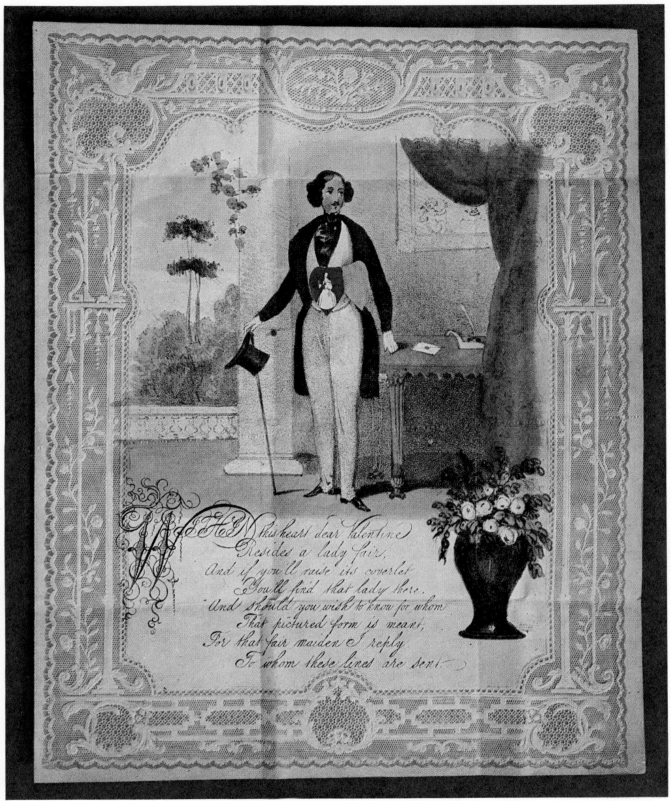

95. **A valentine postmarked in 1846.** The gentleman's waistcoat opens to show his lady love and carries appropriate lines:
"Within this heart dear Valentine Resides a lady fair,
And if you'll raise its coverlet You'll find that lady there.
And should you wish to know for whom That pictured form is meant,
For that fair maiden I reply To whom these lines are sent."

Author's Collection.

96. An exquisite example, quarto size, by Dobbs, Bailey & Co., c. 1850, bright with gaily coloured scraps for ornament. A hand-written message under the lower decoration reads:

"From a disappointed but sincere admirer. We live in Hopes."

Courtesy of W. Bonwitt, London.

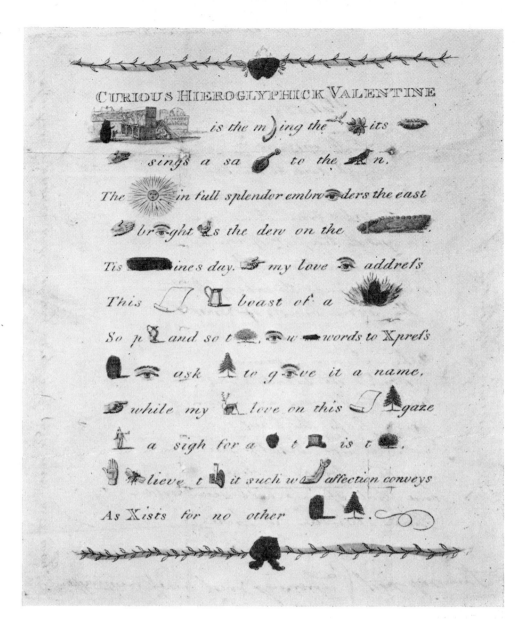

Jonathan King sometimes fall into this category.

A notable manufacturer whose valentines are scarce today was De La Rue & Co. This old-established firm has been in business since 1835 and, until bombed out during the last war, was at 20 Finsbury Place, London. They were well known for their playing cards, and were one of the earliest English firms to manufacture envelopes which, until the advent of a uniform penny postage in 1840, were not in general use. They were also under contract to print some of the postage stamp issues. In 1851 they had a large stand at the Great Exhibition where, to the amazement of a crowd of onlookers, a machine turned out envelopes folded and gummed (a great innovation) at the rate of 3,600 per hour, con-sidered at the time to be a remarkable achievement. De La Rue valentines of this period are very rare; later, after the 1870s, the firm was producing quantities of high-class greetings cards of all descriptions and pub-lished valentines, charmingly designed by very good artists, in chromolithograph.

Messrs. Rock & Co. of Walbrook, London, one of the foremost publishers of pictorial headed writing paper, both serious and comic, also issued valentines in the quarto size. Plate 93 shows one of an amusing series, printed in colour, which they published during the early part of the 1850s. Their valentines were usually of a high standard, and are hard to find. Another of the fancy paper manufacturers whose work is seldom seen was

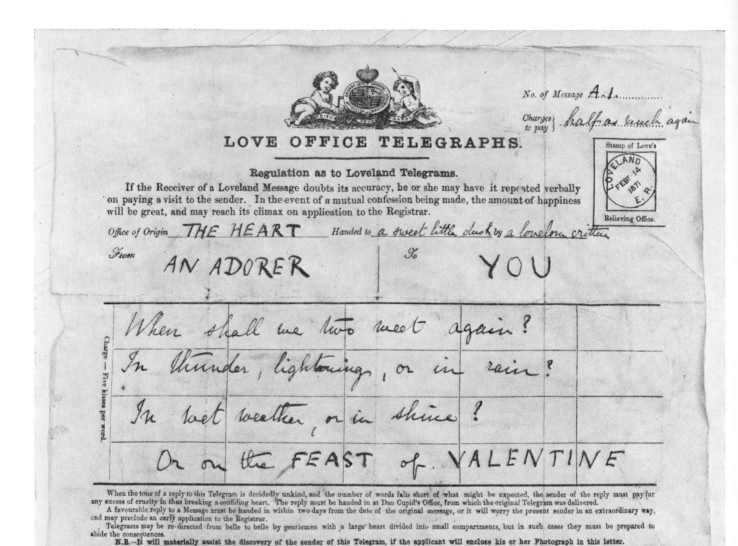

LOVE OFFICE TELEGRAPHS.

Regulation as to Loveland Telegrams.

If the Receiver of a Loveland Message doubts its accuracy, he or she may have it repeated verbally on paying a visit to the sender. In the event of a mutual confession being made, the amount of happiness will be great, and may reach its climax on application to the Registrar.

No. of Message *A. 1.*

Charges to pay } *half as much again*

Stamp of Love's

LOVELAND
FEB. 14
1871
E. R.

Relieving Office.

Office of Origin *THE HEART*　　Handed to *a sweet little duck* by *a lovelorn critter*

From **AN ADORER**　　To **YOU**

Charge — Five kisses per word.

When shall we two meet again?

In thunder, lightning, or in rain?

In wet weather, or in shine?

Or on the FEAST of VALENTINE

When the tone of a reply to this Telegram is decidedly unkind, and the number of words falls short of what might be expected, the sender of the reply must pay for any excess of cruelty in thus breaking a confiding heart. The reply must be handed in at Dan Cupid's Office, from which the original Telegram was delivered.

A favourable reply to a Message must be handed in within two days from the date of the original message, or it will worry the present sender in an extraordinary way, and may preclude an early application to the Registrar.

Telegrams may be re-directed from belle to belle by gentlemen with a large heart divided into small compartments, but in such cases they must be prepared to abide the consequences.

N.B.—It will materially assist the discovery of the sender of this Telegram, if the applicant will enclose his or her Photograph in this letter.

98. Published by Rimmel of the Strand. Printed on pinkish coloured paper, it closely resembled the official telegram of that time—1871. Author's Collection.

Cox & Co. Their work, although pretty to look at, falls far below the standard and quality set by Dobbs, Mansell and others already described.

The 1850s can be said to be a period of transition. Valentines were appearing in ever increasing numbers carrying decoration, often extremely beautiful, but sometimes 'over-done'. Depending on the good taste of the makers they appeared with all manner of novelties. Fine gauze was popular as a background, providing a misty effect for a brightly coloured scrap or some other sort of decoration to show to better advantage. Often the age-old theme of the True-Lover's Knot, or Endless Knot of Love, would be the central motif and, as though perpetuating the former custom of having to look for the message, there were many ingenious ways whereby these loving messages and amorous couplets would be hidden. Sometimes they would be concealed beneath little flaps or inserted under the petals of flowers; minute envelopes, prettily decorated on every flap, would bear tender expressions of love written minutely in careful handwriting. The price asked for this sort of valentine ranged from 1s. 6d. to 4s.

The motif of a lock of hair would be carefully placed underneath a flap of an ornamental envelope so that the ends protruded looking like a drooping moustache. Occasionally, a magnificent lock of hair would ornament or frame the centre piece of the valentine, such as the example shown in Plate 102.

99. A fine example of one of Windsor's smaller valentines, bearing a glass mirror in the centre, c. 1870. Author's Collection.

Realistic bank-notes, cheques and drafts made out by the Bank of True Love, Hymen's Temple, had been published since 1847. A valentine in the shape of a £5 note looked so much like a real Bank of England note that the authorities clamped down on such jokes. The same thing happened in America where imitation dollar bills worded as valentines were very popular, but caused a great deal of embarrassment, so that their publication had to be stopped. The Post Office took objection, too, to the imitation Love Office Telegraph forms which were cleverly printed on pinkish paper to look like the real Post Office telegrams. T. Goode published a number of these in the 1860s, as did Rimmel in 1871.

The traditional gift of a pair of gloves for St. Valentine's Day was kept alive by appropriate verses accompanying not only miniature gloves made of paper and stuck to the valentine card, but sometimes by valentines made up in the shape of a full-sized pair of paper gloves, bearing a message.

It is recorded how, in different parts of the Kingdom, the young lady first sighted as a young man's Valentine, expected the gift of a pair of gloves from him, for her to wear on the following Easter Sunday. In Devonshire it used to be said:

> Good morrow, Valentine, I go today
> To wear for you what you must pay
> A pair of gloves next Easter Day.

100. Valentines in the form of a bank note appeared in 1847. Similar imitations were made in America to look like dollar bills. Author's Collection.

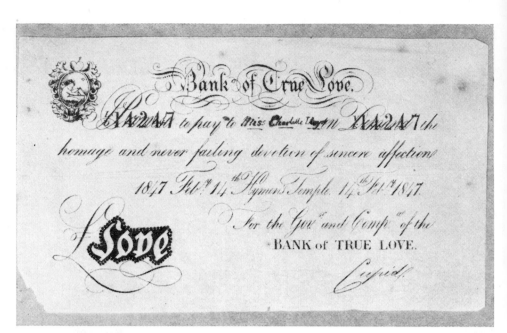

101. A quarto-size valentine on paper by De La Rue & Co. The centrepiece contains a minute envelope with a message inside. Author's Collection.

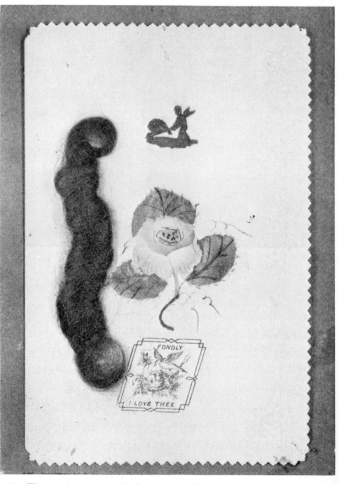

102. This valentine, which carries the simplest of ornaments in the way of a small gilded scrap of Cupid pushing a wheel barrow, a very plainly designed rose and a simple message, is obviously home made. The *pièce de résistance* is the magnificent lock of hair which immediately attracts the attention. Courtesy of the American Antiquarian Society.

103. A pair of gloves enclosed within a decorated envelope. In between the gloves is this verse:
"In friendship as in Love's great pleasure triflings bring,
And many a pair of Gloves are prelude to a Ring."
Author's collection.

And as late as 1849, in Oxfordshire, the custom was still much alive, as is shown by this little rhyme:

> The rose is red, the violet's blue,
> The gillyflower is sweet, and so are you.
> These are the words you bade me say,
> For a pair of new gloves on Easter Day.

Little fancy envelopes came on the market with a pair of tiny paper gloves inside. Often the message would be:

> If that from Glove, you take the letter G
> Then Glove is Love and that I send to thee.

This little couplet is a memory of an older one published as early as 1598, which says:

> Love, to thee I send these gloves,
> If you love me,

> Leave out the G,
> And make a pair of Loves.

Valentines continued to be published in ever increasing numbers over the following twenty years or so, and were made up in every conceivable fashion; some, exquisitely beautiful and costly, others sentimentally lovely, or plainly pretty and catering for all tastes and pockets. There was every sort of comic variety obtainable; many were quite amusing, but some were downright vulgar and almost pornographic. It is a pity, therefore, that despite the great number of novelties and the many different types that came on the market, the charming link with the age-old custom of giving gloves on the 14th of February seems to have lapsed altogether, and it is to be regretted that it has never been revived.

104. A striking envelope, of a sort published by Jonathan King in the 1860s; an imitation wedding ring, fixed by paper, came through the post without damage. Courtesy of A. R. Alcock, Cheltenham.

105. A beautiful and very rare example of an envelope in colour, dated 1864. Author's Collection.

JONATHAN KING: ESTHER HOWLAND

IN the vast collection of ephemera formed by the late Dr. Johnson of Oxford[1] are some of the old sample books which contain the patterns and designs to be stamped out for lace paper, or for embossing. In one album are a few sheets of minute coloured ornaments, perfectly printed and arranged in rows ready for stamping out in embossed shape. It is indeed unfortunate that so little remains to tell us of the art of the early English fancy paper manufacturers, especially of those who made the scraps and ornaments, for later, sometime after the 1860s, much of this beautiful work was supplanted by coloured scraps made in Germany, especially Bavaria.

Many of the better paper makers inserted their name in their paper by means of a watermark, which often showed the year it was made. This is sometimes useful in determining the date of a valentine which happens to be undated either by the postmark or by the person who gave it. However, an actual date cannot be fixed by a paper's watermark, although it establishes the fact that the valentine was used later than the year shown in the watermark.

The paper makers sold their paper to the fancy stationers, who embossed or decorated it either in lace work or by printing. Some of Dobbs's work has been seen on paper made by Smith & Allnutt, 1821, by John Hall and by Joynson, 1842, but much of the paper they used shows no watermark of the maker's name. Similarly, some of Mansell's work is found on paper bearing the watermark of Towgood, in the 1850s. Another name which is often seen is J. Whatman, usually on valentines bearing no name of the publisher.

[1] At the time of writing, plans are under way to move this wonderful collection to the Bodleian Library.

Although several of the fancy stationers made their own valentines, they also sold their fancy paper to others to make up into valentines in any way they pleased, and much of it was sold to the valentine makers in America. A large business flourished, too, in the sale of finished valentines for the American market, when every conceivable sort of valentine, ranging from the sublimely beautiful to the ridiculously comic, was shipped over in quantity as shown by an advertisement which appeared in the *Boston Transcript* of February 9, 1847:

English Valentines, Per *Hibernia*
A. S. Jordan, No. 2 Milk Street, respectfully informs his friends that he has received by the above steamer, the greatest assortment of Valentines to be found in Cupid's regions, among which may be found the following kinds: Comic, Sentimental, Lovesick, Acrostic, Funny, Burlesque, Curious, Characteristic, Humorous, Beautiful, Heart-struck, Witty, Arabesque, Courting, Serio-Comical, Bewitching, Poetical, Heart-rending, Love-encouraging, Trifling, Caricature, Heart-piercing, Serio-tragical, Laughable, Silly, Spiteful, Original, Enlivening, Heart-aching, Despairing, Raving-mad, Heart-killing, High-flown, Lampooning, Romantic, Look-out, Proposal, Espousal, Matrimonial, Hen-pecking, Suicidal, and many other varieties. Wholesale buyers would do well to call before purchasing elsewhere, as the selection has been made by one of the first London houses engaged in that particular business.

There was, besides, a big demand for valentines in the Colonies, especially in Australia, where gold miners, flush with newly acquired wealth from the Ballarat gold mines were willing to pay from £10 to £25 apiece for elaborately assembled valentines such as the one shown in Plate 108. Merchants in Sydney and Melbourne would

106. A typical Esther Howland valentine, showing the very high standard of her work; having a satin back and German made centre ornaments, the whole is mounted upon exquisite embossed paper. Circa 1850s. Courtesy of Carroll Alton Means, Connecticut.

send in orders for this kind of valentine worth a thousand pounds at a time. Extravagant valentines made of a sort of satin cushion, perfumed, ornamented with swansdown, cambric flowers with brightly coloured shells, and adorned with a stuffed humming bird or a bird of paradise, all within a decorated box, were considered highly fashionable and were very expensive.

Elsewhere, English manufacturers of fancy stationery, especially decorated writing paper, and writing paper and cards with embossed or lacy edging, found a ready market for their wares from places not only in Europe, but almost everywhere in the world, for there was none better.

Of all the well-known names associated with the valentine business, in England as well as in America, two stand out above all others. These are Jonathan King of London, and Esther Howland of Worcester, Massachusetts.

Jonathan King was a small-time stationer who, in 1845, opened a little shop at 45 Chapel Street, Somerstown, not far from King's Cross. He sold newspapers and tobacco, carrying stationery and valentines as a sideline, as well as material for juvenile drama and toy theatres. Buying the paper from any one of the many big stationers, his wife Clarissa designed and made up valentines which were sold wholesale as well as retail. Jonathan King was actually a pioneer in the field of decorative lace-paper valentines and devised many unusual designs; his wife was so deft that she could skilfully construct intricate fancy coloured garlands and wreaths consisting of many pieces in half the time it would take anyone else. Mrs. King is accredited with being the first to have the idea, in 1846, of applying tinsel, feathers and birds to valentines, and a few years later, of using glittering tinsel on cards, simply by powdering broken coloured glass. In 1848 Jonathan King's twelve-year-old son, also named Jonathan, started work in the little business, which did so well that the family moved to larger premises in Seymour Street, Euston Square. In the course of time young Jonathan married, and in 1861 brought his bride to his own home and business at 22 Stevenson Terrace, where, whilst he worked as traveller for his father, his young wife looked after the business.

Jonathan King Senior died in 1869 and the two businesses afterwards moved to Islington, where in two villas in Essex Road, Jonathan King and his wife Emily

107. Very fine hand-coloured lithograph on quarto-size paper made by Meek, c. 1840–1850, probably American. Courtesy of Carroll Alton Means, Connecticut.

Elizabeth established themselves in 'The Fancy Valentine Shop' under his wife's name, E. E. King. Alongside the two villas a factory was constructed for the manufacture of greetings cards and valentines, and stationery. Here, in a long work-room and under the supervision of his eldest daughter, Ellen Rose King, some thirty women and girls were kept busy twelve hours or so every day for months on end, making valentines entirely by hand. Wearing aprons, the girls sat at long wooden tables. In front of each was a glue pot and brush, a small pair of scissors, a sharp pen-knife and some miniature pliers. Each girl was supplied with a small fat stock-book which contained a selection of all the many different kinds of scraps and, on the inside cover, a written list of the contents and value.

108. A boxed valentine, two feet in length, made up of hundreds of different coloured scraps, cambric flowers, trinkets and ribbons, against a background of silk and embossed paper: mounted on paper springs, the effect was three-dimensional. This sort of valentine sold well in the Ballarat gold fields. Courtesy of the London Museum (Jonathan King Collection).

109. Artificial flowers and a Humming Bird assembled on a background of swansdown, and mounted within a tasteful box. The flower buds are of little glass beads, and the leaves are made of feathers cut to shape. Courtesy of R. A. Smith, Bath.

It has sometimes been said that the making of valentines was a sweated labour; for a girl, depending on her ability, was paid from 5s. to 15s. a week and worked from 8 o'clock in the morning until 7 o'clock at night. This much is known from a description given of Mansell's manufactory in Charles Dickens's magazine *All The Year Round* (*see* Appendix III), and, remembering how Dickens always supported and championed the poorer people, it would seem that, generally speaking, conditions were tolerably happy and the pay, for those times, not unreasonable.

A trained girl's most useful and important tool, it used to be said, was her 'gum finger', the third finger of each hand which, with amazing speed and dexterity did the job of sticking the finer and more delicate work, the brush being used mainly for the coarser work. The materials which were used, apart from the scraps, were the finest quality rice paper, ribbon, silver lace paper which cost £15 a ream, velvet, satin, swansdown, feathers, shells, pressed ferns and leaves, miniature artificial flowers, as well as perfume to scent them. Sometimes valentines would be heavily decorated with small cambric roses or pheasants' feathers. The cambric roses were imported from France, from a convent where the nuns made them; but people wondered at times at the supposedly high life enjoyed by the King family when they saw so many pheasants delivered at their shop every week!

Nothing was too fantastic or intricate for the King business to tackle. In some of his most beautiful designs

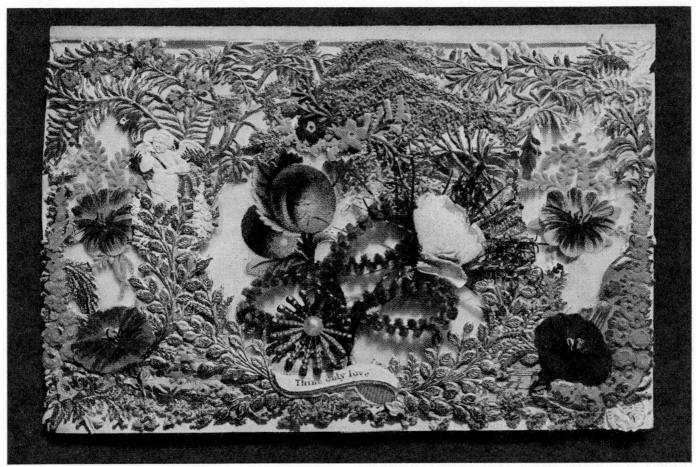

110. Jonathan King exhibited such novelties at the Exhibition of 1862. Made up of gilded wire and tinsel, this sort of colourful valentine was something of a sensation. Author's Collection.

there would be as many as seven hundred separate pieces stuck to a card; but the prize example was the special valentine made by his mother for a very important customer. This consisted of three thousand pieces!

Half a guinea was a usual price to pay for an expensive valentine, and when it is considered that each petal of every flower in an elaborate garland was put on separately, and each feather of a bird's wing or tail was arranged by hand—with appropriate verses and prettily worded couplets all handwritten—this was very reasonable.

Young girls, beginning as apprentices, made the paper 'springs', the small hinges of folded card that held the main or upper part of a valentine away from its base. Some of these valentines, when arranged in a box with their ornamentation displayed in this way, were indeed very lovely. It has been said that paper springs were 'invented' about this time. Actually, in the 18th century,

paper springs were used in religious 'valentines', which were boxed within a small glass-fronted case, often highly ornamental and bejewelled with tinsel and trinkets.

The valentines, apart from the boxed ones made by Jonathan King from the 1860s onwards, were mainly the smaller, octavo size, for since the 1850s the large elegant quarto size had gradually gone out of use mainly due to the conventional sized envelopes which suited a smaller sized valentine.

As well as the usual sentimental kind, Jonathan King published a great variety of humorous valentines and was fond of making use of pictorial puns, and of words with a double meaning. This kind of humour, although sometimes very lame, was well suited to the sort of person for whom it was intended. It is said that Mr. King's elder sons were constantly on the look out for puns which could be written on valentines. An elaborate embossed valentine would show the under part of a very

87

111. One of Jonathan King's advertisements printed on valentine paper, bearing a small diamond-shaped Registration number instead of the maker's name (*see* centre top right). Author's Collection.

Postmasters are now prohibited from aiding any attempt to conceal from those to whom letters are addressed the knowledge of the place from where they originate—which knowledge is, under ordinary circumstances, obtainable from the postmark. Accordingly a number of valentines which have been sent this year to country postmasters at a distance from the place where they were written, with a request that they might be posted at those remote offices, have been sent to the dead letter office, and thence to the parties for whom they were destined, accompanied with a statement showing where the valentines were written, and the means that had been taken to elude detection.

King's output was enormous, and much of his ornamentation and decoration showed great ingenuity. At the time of the Exhibition of 1862, he introduced little model baskets as part of the design, which would be filled tastefully with a colourful spray of artificial flowers—and not only baskets, but miniature vases and bowls. He took great care over his decoration, using fine net frill as edging to cover the embossing or lacework of the paper, so that the whole effect was very pleasing. Metal trinkets and small artificial jewels, pieces of tinsel and fine wire to glitter and catch the eye, surrounded by tinted embossed paper cleverly and prettily decorated with silver and gilt, rendered one of these little valentines a veritable work of art. His decoration at times tended to be on the heavy side, but the general effect was good and suited the taste of those days. His valentines showing the little model baskets are keenly sought after by collectors. One of his more expensive types which sold for 10s. 6d. was The Musical Valentine, which consisted of a love song of four pages with words and music, inside a tastefully printed cover.

An extraordinary type of humorous valentine which King published in several forms had little switches and birches as the central motif, made of small splinters of cane and twigs of heather. The messages were sometimes in the form of puns:

Something to tickle my fancy
A little Corrective
To be applied when the patient is troublesome or naughty.

They would seem to have been in sets, for two others appear on extremely beautiful embossed paper of Dobbs, Kidd & Co. One of these has a coloured scrap of a sheaf

old boot, having a daintily written inscription around it, "You are a good old *Sole*—as ever trod". Another, written in gilt letters on a neat little slate, reads: "Can you cypher, dear? Yes, dear—I sigh for you."

Jonathan King catered for every class of person; he sold not only to individual shoppers but also to the trade, and had agents all over the country. Not only the simple and sometimes poorer class bought from him; the rich and the famous drove up to his door in their carriages. A room set apart was available for special customers, particularly ladies who wished to choose in private. For secrecy was an important factor in the valentine world; even the Post Office, which frowned on taking part in such matters would sometimes forget its officialdom, at least in the smaller offices, and would help by smudging a postmark to help a valentine's anonymity. How strongly the Post Office felt about this is shown in the G.P.O. order issued early in 1857:

112. Valentine in the form of a marriage licence, 1861. Author's Collection.

of oats; above is written in a careful hand, "I fear you will not be worth much without a thrashing", whilst beneath the scrap is written very small, "A hint to my particular friend" (Plate 114). The second variety has a scrap of a large pickle jar bearing a label "Something to pickle". Underneath the jar is a very small twig of heather in the shape of a birch rod, with the message "Something to pickle, I'll give it you".

The factory in Essex Road also produced some very fine valentines in the form of boxes, in which a highly decorated valentine resplendent with gaily coloured scraps, flowers, gold and silver embossed foil, and mounted on laced paper, would fill the entire box but would show as three dimensional, being mounted on paper springs. Some were extremely ornate, and a specimen in the London Museum is nearly two feet in length by about nine inches, and three inches deep. This elaborate valentine is a veritable showpiece of artificial flowers and coloured moss, tinsel and vari-coloured lace paper, some of it silvered and gilt.

Jonathan King was fond, too, of printing all manner of comic valentines in the shape of official forms, wording them in legal phraseology or in the stilted jargon of an official document. These were popular for practical jokers who would send a lady a marriage licence signed by the Reverend Tiethemtight, or a jury summons to the Court of Matter-of-Money in the County of Eithersex. Likewise he printed various sorts of tickets and invitation cards, always full of witticisms and with a lavish play upon words. A sample of his humour is the following which is printed in cursive style to resemble handwriting:

February 14th

Dear and Fascinating,

A willing captive I have been to your matchless charms and graces;

But alas your charms are sadly faded, and your graces have all fled,

Yet am I wanting in language to adequately express my admiration,

And my wonder is that I could have ever considered you tolerable.

It were vain for me to attempt an eulogy on your wondrous beauty,

Your beauty as a work of art, shows skill in the use of cosmetics,

Have I not thought your voice like angel music or the magic of fairy bells,

Ah, though, to hear your shrill notes as you express your thoughts to your maidens,

Have I not compared your breath to the sweet south that breathes on violets?

Those soft breathings so suggestive of fire, brimstone and a flavour of onions,

If the offer of a loving and faithful heart could find favour in your sweet eyes,

Suspect me not of flattery, far be it from me to throw temptation in your way;

If the love and homage of a life's devotion could ensure to you happiness,

Reassure your mind, that there is no thought in my mind to offer it.

113. An elaborate valentine of the 1870s assembled upon a background of lace paper. Each corner has a knot of blue satin ribbon which matched the central background, bearing coloured scraps and moss tastefully arranged within a wreath of net and silvered ferns. Author's Collection.

Fair lady, were you only to smile on the humblest of your
    many lovers,
Your smile would be to me more disagreeable than hen-
    bane or hemlock;
To receive one approving glance from you what great
    happiness,
Your glance would make me as happy as a mouse in the
    presence of a cat.
Lady, you are now in possession of my feelings, pray
    accept my offer,
I now offer you my sincere thanks if you will kindly
    cease to bother me,
Make me the happiest man in the world by acceding to
    my prayer;
Believe me, there is nothing worries me so much as the
    attentions of a coquet.
I need scarcely say, how I long to see your beautiful and
    graceful caligraphy,
No more, and that you are not in any sense to consider me
    Madame,
          Your devoted Lover,

Not only did he make a success out of his greetings cards and valentine business, but he formed the biggest private collection ever known, and strove to obtain examples of every single type of greetings card. He knew more about greetings cards and their publishers and methods of production than anybody. In 1894 he was referred to by Gleeson White, the editor of *The Studio*, and an authority on art, as "the Collector *par Excellence*", and was encouraged by Mr. White to go on collecting in order that one day the nation might benefit by having such a magnificent collection. Jonathan King continued his collecting, and acquired not only the old sample books and material of many of the old-established fancy stationers, but also the current sample books of material being published. He estimated that he had amassed about one million greetings cards and about thirty thousand valentines.

In 1911 he offered his collection to the British Museum, but they were unable to accept it. A small part of it, consisting of over 100 tinsel pictures, framed, 40 large folio volumes containing about 100 tinsel pictures and 9,000 sheets of prints, was gratefully received by the London Museum.

After his death that same year, the bulk of this amazing collection remained at his warehouse in Essex Road. At different times over the years, a few hundred albums containing greetings cards and valentines, came on the

114. On paper made by Dobbs, Kidd & Co. Behind the sheaf, which lifts up, is another message: "A hint to my particular friend". Author's Collection.

market. Finally, in the 1950s, the larger part of what was left of this wonderful collection was sold, most of it going to America where it formed the nucleus of the Hallmark Historical Collection in Kansas City. It can reasonably be inferred that the majority of unused valentines to be seen in any collection today emanated from the sample books which, from time to time, were dispersed from the Jonathan King collection (*see* Appendix IV).

Valentines produced in America during the 1840s were mainly lithographed and hand-coloured, often very beautiful, with a charm distinct from those made in Britain. Others were woodcuts, or hand-made on decorated paper imported from England. American-made paper was not suitable for embossing or for the intricate stamping out of lace work as it lacked the high quality linen content of the good English-made paper. The

115. An assembly of embossed and lacy paper with an edging of fine net-like gauze. The floral centrepiece is made of vari-coloured cambric flowers and moss mounted within a little wicker basket. A good example from Jonathan King's factory. Author's Collection.

elaborate valentines, with their tasteful arrangement of coloured scraps and novelties such as were made in England, were not at this time being produced in America.

It was left to the enterprise of a young college graduate named Esther Howland to introduce the manufacture of this sort of valentine, and to develop it so successfully that her name became famous, so that today her valentines are notable everywhere and cherished in every collection. Esther Howland was a well-educated young lady who had graduated from Mount Holyoke Seminary, Massachusetts, in 1847. Her father, Southworth A. Howland, was a direct descendant of John Howland who came over in *The Mayflower*. He kept the largest bookstore and stationer's shop in Worcester and was considered a substantial business man. How Esther

came to start the fancy valentine industry in America is one of those chance occurrences which has been so often explained in articles and stories, each one differing a little from the other, that it is considered best to give the story which she herself gave to the representative of the *Boston Globe*. In its issue dated February 14, 1901, Arthur W. Brayley explained how he had the pleasure of meeting Miss Esther Howland, the pioneer maker of valentines in her pretty home in Quincy, and of hearing how she came to establish herself in what was to become such a large industry. Her parents had intended that she should enter the teaching profession, but not long after she graduated a chance event in 1848 altered her plans. Miss Howland related to Mr. Brayley how, in 1848, her father added to his stock a few imported valentines, the first which had ever been seen in Worcester. The newspaper account says:

. . . the bright young girl thought it would be no great task to make even prettier ones than the European love missives and told her folks so. They encouraged her in the idea and although she was greatly handicapped by the scarcity of material with which to work, she demonstrated to her own and to her parents satisfaction that she was capable of fashioning some artistic valentines.

Lithography was in its infancy, and small coloured pictures were valued more highly than they are at present. She bought an assortment of these and a number of fancy envelopes which were embellished with a more or less elaborate scroll work on each corner and which were regarded as the proper stationery at that time.

In making the first valentine, Miss Howland cut the designs from the envelopes and pasted them on an ordinary sheet of paper. This answered for lacework. She then added several coloured pictures from her assortment, scalloped the edges of the sheet, and one of her brothers, who was an accomplished penman, inscribed various verses significant of love.

Taking two or three dozens of these home-made valentines as samples, another brother went to Boston and New York to see if he could get orders for the next season's trade. In two or three weeks he had orders for several thousand dollars worth of them to fill which taxed even her remarkable resourcefulness.

The father went to New York and ordered from a Mr. Snyder, a lithographer, a quantity of small coloured pictures, and then sent to England to a manufacturer of embossed paper for a supply of that material, as none was made in this country. A little room was fitted up in their cosy home, and four or five girls employed.

The next year Miss Howland looked about for novelties and was able to provide her brother with a larger assortment of samples when he started on his canvass. Many of these valentines were quite elaborate and costly and among them were the first valentines of which satin and silk formed a part.

That year the orders were more than doubled, and so was the working force in the factory. A more commodious room was utilised, in which a large table was built, and around the table, the bright young employees, mostly young girls, friends of the family, would gather and copy the designs made by Miss Howland. In time quantities of enamelled coloured pictures and other novelties were imported from Germany, but as these had to be cut out with scissors, the enterprising manufacturer had a set of dies made and used for that purpose. She then conceived the idea of embossing the little lithographic ornaments. She wrote to a firm in Germany telling them of her plan and that she would have the cutting and embossing dies made and sent to them.

But that house knew a good thing when they saw it. They declined Miss Howland's offer but had dies of their own made in Germany at smaller cost. A few months later embossed and cut pictures were on the market, but the only advantage the originator of the idea received was in being able to buy them in more convenient form.

May baskets were also made by the enterprising young woman, and were quite popular in their day. The first very elaborate May basket she made, one that retailed for $10 was bought by a young man and hung on the front door of his fiancée's residence. But when that thrifty miss received it she almost broke the young spendthrift's heart by telling him that a man who was fool enough to pay $10 for a May basket would not suit her for a husband, and straightway dismissed him.

Miss Howland laughingly remarked after relating this incident that she never again made so expensive a May basket.

Gradually the trade expanded and went as far as California, and the business done amounted to $50,000 and $75,000 a year. In the very busiest period, the young woman met with a severe accident.

While on business in Boston she fell on an ice-covered sidewalk and broke her knee-pan. She was confined to her bed several weeks, and then for 3 or 4 years made her designs and superintended her large and constantly growing business while seated in a wheel chair.

It was considered quite a privilege to work for Miss Howland, for she paid liberally, and the work was light

116. Miss Esther Howland, a photograph taken about 1860. Taken from the *Boston Globe* of February 14, 1901.

117. This valentine by Esther Howland was one of her specials. Consisting of seven pages, each one carefully ornamented with scraps and embossed paper, it sold for $30. Courtesy of Hallmark Historical Collection.

118. A beautiful example of Esther Howland's work. Courtesy of Hallmark Historical Collection.

and pleasant, while only such girls as were known to her were allowed to join their circle.

She was always fond of the society of young girls, so much so that she took care of four bright young misses whose parents had met with business reverses, and brought them up as members of her household, and they remained with her until they married.

A remarkable feature of the valentine business at that time was that Miss Howland had no competition, except the foreign importations. She monopolised the business in the United States. One large company in New York whose order almost doubled each year until it amounted to $25,000 made her a liberal offer to control her goods. Failing in which they tried to buy her business, but both offers were declined.

But what money could not do, filial love accomplished. Her father met with an accident and required constant attention. She considered that her place was at her aged father's side, that she could administer to his wants and care for him better than strangers, but in doing so she must give up the business. It did not take her long to decide between the two.

Among those employed by her was Mr. George C. Whitney, and when she decided to discontinue the business he bought her out.

A distinguishing idea of Esther Howland's which remained her own for a long time was to use coloured glazed paper wafers as backing behind the embossing for her cards. The coloured background which they made caused the embossing and lace work in the design to show up to better advantage. Very likely she got this idea from the way some English valentines were finished by being interleaved with coloured pieces of tissue paper between the embossed or paper lace work, which showed up the work so attractively. Often these coloured paper wafers, such as used by her—measuring about $\frac{1}{2}$ inch to 1 inch in diameter—were placed one in each corner of a valentine, rendering a very pleasing effect.

This is a means whereby collectors can distinguish American valentines from English, and Howland's from other American valentines. For, many years later, when she had relinquished her business, other American firms copied her styles. Manufacturers were always on the look-out for new ideas, but when using the ideas of others, they invariably attempted to alter them in such a way as to be distinguishable from their own productions.

In common with Jonathan King and other valentine manufacturers in England, she bought her supplies of embossed and lace paper, blanks, etc., from the best makers, from firms such as Mansell, Wood, Meek and others. At first she followed the English style of assembling, but later she introduced the idea of several paper-lace motifs one on top of the other, with pieces to lift up, and as an added attraction, usually a small coloured picture as a centrepiece. Not liking the use of little scraps bearing printed messages to be on the front of her valentines she had slips of paper with the usual verses and couplets neatly printed, stuck on the inside page.

Her valentines were always made in the best taste, and were considered most superior. Some were very costly, too, selling at $5 and $10 each. It is related how, when she first started and before her business grew so large, she would personally inspect every valentine made on the premises.

Because of the high cost of lace paper, some valentine manufacturers attempted to make their own dies. Esther

119. A very fine example of Esther Howland's work on two quarto sheets made by Kershaw of gold lace paper, hand-tinted with water colour, c. 1860. The boy is in blue and the girl in pink. Courtesy of Carroll Alton Means, Connecticut.

120. A magnificent example of embossing by Berlin & Jones, New York, c. early 1860s. Embellished with coloured scraps and a centrepiece entitled "Friendship's Offering", the printed message is on coloured paper fastened to the inside page. Courtesy of the Metropolitan Museum of Art, New York (Gift of Lee Carter Morse, 1950).

Howland contacted an ingenious die sinker in Worcester, named Andrew Weir, and engaged him to copy some of the simpler English patterns, but his dies being somewhat crude, the attempt was not successful. However, these dies were used for embossing envelopes which can sometimes be found with Howland valentines.

During the 1860s a well-known firm of stationers and envelope manufacturers in New York, Berlin & Jones,

sent one of their men, Jotham W. Taft, to London in order to learn something of the closely guarded secrets of lace-paper making. His adventures are described in a column about valentine making which was written for the New York *World* newspaper in 1877:

Messrs. Berlin & Jones, who used to have a printing establishment at 134 William Street, once formed the plan of manufacturing this paper, and sent over a mechanic named Taft to Europe to make drafts of the machinery employed. Taft had a jolly time, made friends with the lace-paper workmen, and was admitted into the factory, where he made complete drawings when nobody was looking. He was found out when he had finished and was near being mobbed by the indignant manufacturers, but he got away with his sketches and came back to New York.

Here machinery was constituted on the plans which he had brought, but for some reason they would never work, and the manufacture of lace paper still remains a monopoly on the other side—in England and France, and at Leipsic and Nuremberg. Embossed paper, however, is made here in perfection, and also the boxes and trimmings and everything else but the lace paper are turned out in a high state of beauty.

Probably, the main reason for this failure (as well as Esther Howland's attempt) was because of the quality of the paper, and the fact that it lacked a high-grade rag content. For American paper was generally made of wood pulp, and the weakness of the fibres prevented any clean cut away and removal of the paper after its pressing. Some years afterwards, Berlin & Jones, working under a patent (Lang's patent) and copying the English patterns, finally succeeded in making 8vo and 12mo sheets of lace paper.

Sometime during the early part of the 1870s, Esther Howland reorganised her business, and as a result, The New England Valentine Company was formed at 425 Main Street, Worcester. From now on her valentines, envelopes, and other greetings cards (she no longer confined herself only to valentines) were marked with an embossed 'N.E.V. Co.'. Whilst at this address she had a working association with Edward Taft, the son of Jotham W., who is listed in the Worcester directories from 1877 to 1880 as a 'valentine maker' at the same address.[1] Valentines made by him (or his father) bear an embossed 'Taft' on the back. The exact date when Esther Howland sold out to the George C. Whitney Company is not known for certain, but it can safely be conjectured to be about 1880-1881.

George C. Whitney was the youngest of three brothers. Sumner and Edward were engaged individually in making valentines in 1858. The next year they joined forces and were in business together at 218 Main Street, Worcester, as Whitney Bros. The eldest brother died in 1861; George, the youngest, was away serving with the

[1] The History of Valentines by Ruth Webb Lee, Batsford.

121. A typical valentine made by Whitney about 1870. White lace paper is mounted upon a background of green, picked out by red roses. Author's Collection.

55th Regiment of the Massachusetts Volunteers in the Civil War, but joined his brother Edward when he came back from the army in 1865. The two brothers opened up in business together under the name of The Whitney Valentine Co., but a few years later in 1869 Edward left the partnership to start on his own wholesale stationery and paper business in premises next door. George Whitney continued alone manufacturing valentines and became the Whitney Manufacturing Co.

Like all other valentine makers, he imported his lace paper and embossed envelopes from England, and his coloured scraps and ornaments from Germany. His valentines resemble very closely those of Esther Howland, and there is no doubt that he copied from her, even in the method of marking; Whitney's valentines show a small red 'W' stamped on the back, which match Esther Howland's 'H' in size and style. Some bear only a

numeral which probably indicates the price or range. His embossed envelopes bear the embossed imprint 'Whitney, Worcester'.

But it is interesting to observe at this stage how, copying Esther Howland's style, and her original idea of inserting a coloured background to the lace paper with another paper of different colour for each of the four corner pieces, seems to have given Whitney the idea of employing coloured embossed paper and using background paper printed in colour for his valentines. This fashion was soon copied by every other American manufacturer, so that it is difficult for a collector to tell one maker from another, except where a distinguishing mark can be seen. Because of this, American valentines of the 1860s to 1880s period are recognisable at once from those of English manufacture, whilst those of a later date, still following this traditional form of assembly begun by Esther Howland and George Whitney, differ even more so.

Late in the 1860s, George C. Witney bought the A. J. Fisher Company of New York, whose specialty had been the manufacture of comic valentines. Mr. Whitney, it is said, disliked comic valentines intensely and would have nothing to do with them. According to Ruth Webb Lee in *A History of Valentines*, Mr. Whitney offered all the

A. J. Fisher plates and cuts to another manufacturer of comic valentines, McLoughlin Brothers of New York. Continuing to expand, the Whitney business in 1869 took over the old established and important firm of Berlin & Jones of New York. The company now had the need for still larger premises and moved to 393 Main Street in 1874. Next to be taken over was Esther Howland, together with Edward Taft's interest, soon followed by the Bullard Art Publishing Co. of Worcester.

The Whitney empire was now indeed formidable; known as the George C. Whitney Company, and with its headquarters in Union Street, Worcester, it continued for many years as a great concern, with offices in Boston, New York and Chicago. It survived a disastrous fire in 1910, and continued to flourish up to the death of Mr. Whitney in 1915. His son, Warren, carried on the business until 1942, when, due to restrictions and the paper shortage brought about by the war, this huge concern which had started from such small beginnings, was forced to close down.

It is perhaps curious to reflect that, whereas the observance of St. Valentine's Day had practically lapsed in Britain since the time of World War I, in America, the age-old custom of remembering one's sweetheart on the 14th of February had continued unbroken.

LATER VICTORIAN ERA

EARLY in the 1860s Christmas cards began to be used extensively. It cannot definitely be stated when the first popular issues came out, but it is fairly safe to assert that this happened about 1862. The very first Christmas card of all had been published in 1843 by Felix Summerly (the *nom de plume* of Henry Cole) from a design by John Horsley. Only 1,000 were printed, hand-coloured on a card about the size of an ordinary playing card. The development of cheap colour printing had made it possible to produce Christmas cards cheaply and, thanks to the Penny Post, this was an easy and popular way of keeping in touch with friends and relations, so that the public responded eagerly to the new vogue. As a result, many businesses began to publish Christmas cards. and some of the old-established firms in the fancy stationery line, already well known for their valentines, now turned to the printing of Christmas cards as well.

These early type Christmas cards were small, conforming in size to the usual visiting card and playing card, which fitted conveniently into the little envelopes commonly used in those days. Postage was 1d. per ½ ounce, which adequately suited their size and weight.

This was not always the case with valentines. According to the custom, many of the popular styles were in the usual letter-sheet size. These, when sent through the post, would be folded into the conventional size of an envelope, and closed either by wax or by wafer seal. If the valentine was only a printed design, all was well; it came through the post undamaged and incurred no extra postage. But if, as so often was the case, the valentine was ornamented with heavy decoration in the way of spun glass, shells or trinkets, it could be damaged in the post unless carefully packed, and this would incur

additional postage. Whereas extra postage would not bother the sender of an expensive valentine of this sort, it did mean however that their use was more limited.

These large heavily decorated valentines are usually found today in unposted condition, denoting that they were given in person by the sender, or delivered by hand; but it was about this time that decorated and embossed envelopes were being made in larger size to take valentines more easily, a custom that had been in vogue in America for a long time. There, envelopes the size of a letter sheet were commonly used, in order that the valentines need not be folded.

The small Christmas cards, now so very popular, obviously pointed the way to smaller-sized valentines, which would fit conveniently into normal sized envelopes. This in no way led to any reduction in the beauty or amount of decoration. If anything, these smaller valentines often showed an even greater display of artistic arrangement and diversity of ornamentation than the larger ones. Many of the high-class makers such as Dobbs (now Dobbs, Kidd & Co.), Mansell, Meek and others continued to manufacture the quarto size for those who wanted them, and many were so elaborately fashioned that they required to be boxed.

Apart from the names already mentioned, other lace-paper makers and embossers also producing valentines were now coming to the fore, notably Mullord Bros., Goode, Spragg, Sulman and Robert Canton. Mullord Bros. had been in business since the 1840s, and produced very fine high-grade embossed work, with wonderful cameo-like effect. Most of their work is found in smaller sized valentines dating from the 1860s. Goode Brothers was another old-established firm, whose work is more often seen dated during the 1860s. Benjamin Sulman is

123. A beautiful little valentine typical of the heavy adornment of the 1870s. The pansies are made of velvet, the clusters of pearls are set upon satin leaves and the coloured scraps on either side are mounted on pink. The whole is assembled on silk, backed and edged with embossed silvered paper. Author's Collection.

124. A clever advertisement of Robert Canton, who published many humorous rather than comic valentines. Courtesy of Carroll Alton Means, Connecticut.

first heard of in the same decade and produced delightfully engraved and embossed cards. His cards were usually small, about the size of a visiting card, beautifully embossed with fancy edges. Robert Canton had been well known since the 1840s for small prints, and now that valentines were popular in small size he produced embossed lace-paper valentines (although it is said that the intricate lace borders were actually made by Meek) with printed rhymes.

All these firms made Christmas cards, too, and frequently the same designs would be used either for Christmas or St. Valentine's Day.

A great novelty of the 1860s was the introduction of perfumed sachets. Generally these were made of a material similar to cotton wool impregnated with an essence of perfume, lavender and violet being very popular. This was padded and enclosed within a heavily decorated envelope made of embossed paper, usually silvered, but sometimes coloured and ornamented with small scraps and bearing a prettily worded message of affection. Several firms made them, but Rimmels of the Strand is the firm principally associated with them (see Appendix V). Eugene Rimmel, with branches in New York and Paris, specialised in perfumed sachets. Rimmel's sachets were contained within beautifully decorated envelopes. The padded sachet, itself enclosed within a prettily ornamental cover, would be stuck to the centre of the envelope whose flaps would be open to reveal a dainty picture with an appropriately worded couplet. These cost from 6d. to 10s. 6d. each. Another firm, making a specialty of perfumed sachets of a different sort, was Thomas Stevens of Coventry. In the style of a small valentine, and contained within an elaborate assembly of embossed paper and ornament, a little sachet would be inset as a central motif. But, vastly different from any other, the message it carried would be woven in coloured silks. These were advertised in Stevens's price list for 1870 at 2s. 6d. to 21s. per dozen; valentines for 1870, described as: "An Extensive Variety of Floral and other kinds, with Patent Woven Illuminated Silk Centre mottoes, from 2s. 6d. to 200s. per dozen." Stevens also manufactured (along with a large variety of other subjects), bookmarkers of woven silk suitably worded for St. Valentine's Day which sold for 6d. and 9d. each. These were so popular that the idea was copied by others in the silk trade, and it was not long before they were being manufactured by Welch

125. A beautiful valentine of the 1870s by Mullord Bros. Author's Collection.

126. An embossed envelope in bluish pink and gold, with a centrepiece of woven silk in red and blue saying, "Remember Me". The front opens to reveal a perfumed sachet. On the other side a coloured scrap of floral design conceals another centre of woven silk with the message, "May our Hearts be united in Love for ever". Probably made by Stevens of Coventry, c. 1870. Courtesy W. Bonwitt, London.

and Lenton of Coventry, Grants of Leamington, and others. Today, these woven silk book markers are hard to find and keenly collected.

In America the tragic years of the Civil War brought forth a new fashion in writing paper and stationery. Envelopes and writing paper came to be printed in huge quantities and often in full colour, embellished with patriotic and political motifs. There were those that were sentimental, showing sweethearts taking leave of their loved ones; some expressed loyalty for popular heroes and generals; others carried political skits, and many were comic.

Valentines, too, were published along these lines. All are rare today and collectors pay big prices for any that chance to turn up at auction. Charles Magnus of 12 Frankfurt Street, New York, was one of the biggest publishers of Civil War patriotic stationery. He also published ballads and love songs as pictorial letter sheets with coloured headings. Many of these, by reason of their sentimental purpose, were used as valentines. Charles Magnus also published valentine sheets, both serious and comic (*see* Plate 130).

An amusing Civil War valentine by an unknown publisher is shown in Plate 131.

> "A Regular"
> My love is a regular man—
> A man with a regular way;
> He means to regulate me—if he can,
> When he gets his regular pay.
> But I'll be no regular's wife,
> No! no! not for all creation;
> For who could enjoy married life,
> When bound to a mere regulation.

More serious is the very popular valentine shown in Plate 129. Although many copies are seen in different collections, it is one that always fetches a high price in the sale room.

Both in England and in America, comic valentines continued to be published in large quantities, to supply a popular demand. In England in the 1870s some of these comic valentines, cheaply printed in colour on poor paper were being produced in sheets, sometimes measuring as much as 30 inches long.

They were not always in the best of taste, and they surely caused distress to those unfortunate enough to receive them. So many were cruel in their humour and

127. A book-marker of woven silk, by T. Stevens of Coventry, c. 1870. Author's Collection.

others were extremely vulgar. Many a young lady was rendered unhappy by receiving a valentine telling her that she was considered 'boss-eyed' and a young man would be made to feel very uncomfortable on getting a valentine sent to a 'snake in the grass'. But this kind of valentine persisted.

Whereas the old-established firms continued to produce beautiful valentines in traditional style, assembled by hand on lace paper and embellished with all manner of attractive little ornaments, there was now a tendency for valentines to be decorated with heavier and more solid ornaments; it was a change in fashion. During the 1870s valentines were embellished with beads, sea shells, fir cones, dried berries and seeds of all kinds

103

128. Wrapper for a packet of Civil War valentines. Courtesy of Norcross Collection, New York.

brightly coloured, sometimes set among moss and sea weed which had been dyed in many hues. In the midst of all this decoration, artificial flowers made of cambric and velvet were ingeniously arranged, and the whole *ensemble* could be displayed to better advantage by having its many pieces mounted on paper springs so that when raised, the effect was three dimensional. Smaller valentines, too, were becoming increasingly popular, usually about four inches by three in size but sometimes smaller; even one inch by one-and-a-half but, so small as these, were either in the form of novelties or for children. The small valentines were also boxed and, displayed with all the paper springs raised, looked very attractive, the better quality ones being placed in decorated boxes.

At first, sometime about the 1850s, very small scraps (made in Germany) bearing love messages, were added to the decoration, but now they sometimes featured as a centre piece, either in the form of a cluster of flowers or showing a pretty young lady, or in some other attractive way, and were often the predominant feature.

Applying dress material to the pictures, such as satin or brocade to make the dresses realistic, became popular and the flounced dresses and crinolines were charmingly fashioned in this way, whilst gentlemen's styles would be shown in cloth. Movable novelties, in which, on lifting the principal part something totally different was revealed that would change the picture's motif, and others of a kind shown in Plates 133 and 134 were great favourites.

Doubtless the tremendous popularity of Christmas cards played a great part in the gradual change that was about to take place with valentine designs and styles. Ever since their inception Christmas cards, having evolved from the usual size and shape of a visiting card, had more or less remained about the size of a playing card.

The early types of Christmas cards were generally lithographed and hand-coloured and, with the great advances made in colour printing and the introduction of cheap designs imported from Germany, they were very inexpensive. One penny was quite an ordinary price to pay for a card. This was in sharp contrast to the price of valentines which, usually hand-made and far more elaborate, would cost from sixpence upwards (for small ones), although the comic sort, cheaply printed in colour, cost only a penny. It was natural that there should be a gradual change in the size and price of valentines.

By now, one or two firms were established in the colour printing business specializing in chromolithography, who were to become famous for the beautiful greetings cards they published. Foremost was Marcus Ward of Belfast, who opened a branch in London in 1867. Already engaged in the Christmas card business, the company published valentines too, and was well known for having 'discovered' a gifted young artist, Kate Greenaway. Kate Greenaway was only twenty-two years old when she exhibited some drawings at the first Black and White Exhibition held at the Dudley Gallery, Egyptian Hall, in Piccadilly in 1868. Her drawings of fairy scenes and children attracted the attention of the Revd. W. J. Loftie, editor of the *People's Magazine*, who was so charmed with them that he paid the modest sum of £2 2s. od. for a frame of six, and contacted her. This acquaintance with Mr. Loftie can be said to have given Kate Greenaway her chance, for he was instrumental in giving her work and was able to recommend her to Kronheim & Company, the colour printers for whom she did a number of drawings.

It was about this time, early in the 1870s, that Messrs. Marcus Ward, when considering plans for the extension of their business, became interested in an idea which Mr. Loftie had given them for publishing artistic Christmas cards and valentines. Kate Greenaway's work was brought to the notice of Mr. Marcus Ward who was immediately attracted by her particular style of drawing children in late 18th-century costume and with her application of mediæval ornament.

The first work she did for Marcus Ward & Co, was a valentine which turned out to be such a great success that, within a few weeks, upwards of 25,000 copies were sold. Although her own reward was little more than £3, she continued with the firm for some years at the same low remuneration, designing not only valentines but Christmas cards and New Year's cards as well. The extraordinary thing about this highly successful effort is that no one today apparently has seen a copy, although so many were made!

129. A very popular valentine of the Civil War. The picture, showing a soldier writing to his wife, is enclosed by the flaps of the tent, which open out. Author's Collection.

130. Published by Charles Magnus, c. 1862. Courtesy of Norcross Collection, New York.

131. A pleasant valentine of the Civil War, dated 1865. Inscriptions written on by the recipient always give a personal touch and bring a valentine 'to life'. Courtesy of Norcross Collection, New York.

132. A scarce valentine, which cost two cents when it was published in about 1860, by the New York Union Valentine Co. Courtesy of Hallmark Historical Collection.

Kate Greenaway's drawings of children have never failed to give pleasure; in their old-fashioned pretty dresses they have a charm and style all their own and, despite her many imitators, a genuine Kate Greenaway design is quite easily recognised, although her early efforts do not bear her simple signature—K.G. One set of her valentines, however, is distinctly different from all others. These are the illustrations which, together with those done by Walter Crane, appeared in a beautiful volume of verses called *The Quiver of Love, a collection of valentines, Ancient and Modern*. This delightful book was published in 1876, and contains four illustrations by Kate Greenaway and four by Walter Crane. They were all published separately as valentines, usually with the verses printed on the back of the cards, but sometimes two cards would be joined together, like a folder, so that the verse showed opposite the picture. It is generally believed that the verses were by Mr. Loftie. Some cards were published with a fine lace edging; others were scalloped, whilst those made as folders were usually edged with a coloured silk fringe.

Walter Crane's drawings in *The Quiver of Love* are considered by many people, in this instance, to be superior to those of Kate Greenaway who, unlike her later drawings of charmingly dressed little children, had depicted young ladies in mediæval style. It must, however, be remembered that Walter Crane was already an established artist, whereas these four illustrations by Kate Greenaway represent her early work. Even so there are some who contend that it is difficult to tell the two apart, although the illustrations by Walter Crane always have a gold background, whereas those of Kate Greenaway have a designed background.

Another and much smaller volume of *The Quiver of Love* was published in 1880 which had no illustrations at all by Walter Crane but contained four by Kate Greenaway, quite different from those in the original edition.

By the end of the 1870s Kate Greenaway was well known and had become an illustrator for several magazines and papers. But it is as an illustrator of children's books that she became famous and, as in the case of *The Quiver of Love*, some of these appeared separately as valentines. Of these, the following are most sought after by collectors: from the book *A Cruise in the Acorn*—one illustration, from *Melcomb Manor*—a set of six illustrations, and from *Puck and Blossom*—also a set of six. There were series of cards too: *The Children on Flowers, The Children by the Pond* and *The Forging of the Ring*. The sets consisted of four cards, but in the last named there might have been six. They are difficult to come by.

Several of Marcus Ward's chromolithographs are on cards having a beautiful lace paper edging, which would seem to be a transitional stage between the frilly lace-paper valentines which had for so long been the fashion, and the pictorial valentines which so closely resembled Christmas cards. *Punch* in January 1880 comments on the enormous output of Christmas cards and gently condemns them as a nuisance, in much the same way as people do today. Under the title: *More Cards Already*, Mr. Punch says:

> The mighty MARCUS, scarcely breathed
> From sleet of Christmas card,
> In card-house of St. Valentine
> Holds us again at WARD!

Grumbling in several verses of this sort Mr. Punch points out how, no sooner is the sleet of Christmas cards over than, three weeks in advance, their valentines, "With Hearts and Darts and Loves and Doves, and Floating Fays and Flowers", are on the market!

Another name which quickly came to the fore and was eventually to become noted for good quality and high standard was that of Raphael Tuck. Raphael Tuck came from Breslau where, unsettled by the Prusso-Danish and the Austrian war of 1864-66, he hopefully came to England for a fresh start. Beginning very modestly in 1866 in a small business of his own where he sold pictures and did picture framing, he founded the firm which was ultimately to become Raphael Tuck & Sons Ltd. From selling and framing pictures, and thanks to the untiring work of his wife and three sons, they moved to larger premises and entered the field of pub-

133. This kind of valentine was very popular in the 1870s; One picture conceals another which gives quite a different meaning to the card. Author's Collection.

134. Comic valentine by Mansell of the 'movable' sort. By pulling the tag the lady's crinoline disappears to reveal her undergarments. Author's Collection.

lishing, producing chromolithographs, oleographs and black and white lithographs. In 1871 the firm published their first Christmas cards and expanded so rapidly that, by 1880 their name had become a household word. During the 1880s they published many valentines, especially attractive novelties such as the beautiful fan shown in Plate 143. Later they were making the mechanical 'stand-ups' such as were being imported by other businesses from Germany. These were novelties, which, although folded flat, could be raised and made to stand up, including such articles as carriages, ships and all manner of whimsical attractions, ornamented with hearts and cupids.

In keen competition too was the old-established firm of De La Rue and Co.; whereas their Christmas cards are frequently seen, their valentines do not turn up so often. A charming example is shown in Plate 138.

An important contemporary in the field of chromolithography was Louis Prang who improved the technique of lithography to perfection. Born in Breslau in 1824 he, like Raphael Tuck, not liking the political state of affairs in his own country and wishing for better opportunities, emigrated to the United States in 1850. He was first in business as a lithographer in partnership with Julius Mayer in 1856, but four years later the partnership was dissolved and he started on his own in Roxbury, a suburb of Boston, as L. Prang & Company. Constantly improving his technique, he became so expert in chromolithography that it was difficult sometimes to distinguish his reproductions from originals and his work was greatly admired by experts in the trade on both sides of the Atlantic. In 1874 he published his first Christmas card and then entered into the greetings card business on a large scale, so much so that he became known as the 'Father of the American Christmas Card', and took his place along with Esther Howland and George C. Whitney as a pioneer in the American greetings card industry. Up till then, Christmas cards had been regularly imported into the U.S.A. from Europe, especially from England. Now his productions were not only enjoyed in America, but were also exported to Europe where his cards were recognised and appreciated for the excellence of their design and reproduction. He published valentines, too, but whereas his Christmas cards are fairly easy to come by, valentines bearing the imprint 'Copyright L. Prang & Co. Boston' are not so easily found.

135. A Walter Crane design, one of a set of four which appear in *The Quiver of Love,* a volume of valentine verses, published by Marcus Ward & Company in 1876. Courtesy of Hallmark Historical Collection.

136. A very beautiful example published by **Louis Prang** of Boston, with a fringe of coloured silk, considered very elegant in the 1880s. Courtesy of the Hallmark Historical Collection.

At this time there was already a perceptible decline in the popularity of valentines, more so in England than in America, and this would account for the market in the mechanical and trick types of valentines which catered more for younger people and for children. Comic valentines, too, were commonly vulgar and compared unfavourably with the general good taste of the Christmas card.

Commenting on valentines in general the New York newspaper *World* in 1878 said:

Tomorrow is the festival of St. Valentine. The post

office people say that, as far as the mails are concerned, the business of the day is nothing like what it used to be four or five years ago. The bulk of valentines which the clerks handle go to Ireland and Germany, whither the servant girls of America send them as easy substitutes for difficult letters, and as tasteful matters likely to please the people at home. The stamp of the mailing clerk, coming down in the indiscriminating rush of his occupation upon the cover of a pasteboard box, spoils only a small section of the delicate favour written, and it goes on its way thereafter pretty happily.

The dealers in valentines, in contradiction of the post office people, say that the business is more enormous than ever. The issue this year is estimated at 30,000 gross, and almost the entire manufacture of these is monopolized by the two New York houses of the McLoughlin Brothers and A. J. Fisher. . . . A. J. Fisher makes some of the most costly valentines, and sells his best for $50 apiece. McLoughlin Brothers have a large factory in Williamsburg, where they turn out a great deal of fine work, and enormous quantities of those 'comics'—the sort that sell for 1 cent apiece. The manufacture of these goes on all the year round. . . .

Many manufacturers in Germany produced attractive valentines during the 1880s and 1890s, but not all bear the names of established businesses; they merely carry the imprint: "Printed in Germany". For the most part these were the 'trick' and 'mechanical' types of valentines which were in demand both in England and in America around the years 1890 and 1900. Although flat when closed, or in a box, these were so ingeniously made of folded card, that all the parts when pressed out assembled themselves into a standing model such as the delightful example shown in Plate 147. One German firm in particular, E. Nister of Nuremberg, established agencies both in New York and in London and published some charming valentines, as the one shown in Plate 144. Another with a branch in New York was Obpacher Brothers of Munich; their valentines are hard to find. An American firm who produced many delightful valentines in the 1880s was Baldwin Gleason of Boston. Their cards are usually small and in black and white, printed on ivorine, which was one of the few available plastics known in the late 19th century.

A distinguishing mark of some of the more expensive and elegant valentines was the silk fringed edge. This truly Victorian form of decoration had gradually replaced the delicate lace-paper edges which for so long

137. Two cards by Kate Greenaway. Left, An illustration from the book *A Cruise in the Acorn*, by Alice Jerrold; Right, "Children on Flowers", with a verse on the back. Both cards published by Marcus Ward. Courtesy of Carroll Alton Means, Connecticut.

(within left card image)

WITH ALL OUR CANVAS UP,
Primrose and Violet together,
We sail in an acorn cup,
We sail in the summer weather.

WE TALK OF NOTHING BUT LOVE,
Ripples ahead are singing,
White wings flash in the air above,
The rudder ropes are swinging.

"YOU'LL BE MINE AND THINE I'LL BE,
Always and always, ever and ever,"
Thus we sing in a sweet low key,
Sailing down lifes rapid river.

---

had been a feature. From the early 1880s, cards, sometimes single or folded into two, were edged with all sorts of coloured silk fringes, the folded cards usually having silk cords or tassels to make it easier for opening. The fashion seems to have been quick to catch on and was adopted simultaneously by all the leading manufacturers, as well as by Prang in America.

There was now, however, a noticeable decline in the general observance of St. Valentine's Day and there was no longer the fervour or excitement which, in years gone by, used to take place. This was commented on at the annual dinner of the Company of Old English Valentine Makers in London on February 14, 1884.

Among some of the propositions discussed were the following:

1. Is the Valentine custom slowly reviving and is it desirable in the public interest for the press to make it again popular?

2. It is essentially an English trade.

3. The vulgarity of the earlier periods had already been suppressed by all respectable stationers.

4. The ramifications of the trade touched nearly all branches of artistic labour in this country, as follows: Artists, Hand Painters, Die Sinkers, Litho Printers, Letterpress Printers, Drapers, Commercial Travellers, and the rank and file of Embossers, Perforators, Box Makers, Valentine hands, and lastly, Wholesale and Retail Dealers.

As a result of this dinner and the discussions that took place there, Jonathan King printed a two-paged leaflet which was sent to customers and to all concerned in the valentine trade. This leaflet stated that to foster the revival of the valentine custom would be to the benefit of all Fancy Trades especially, and to the nation generally, in a small degree to a particular British industry. It set forth that, among other reasons, valentines died out from a process of natural decay, and that the press con-

111

.TO.
MY LOVE

138. One of a set of three published by De La Rue and Co. in 1879. The centres are coloured against a silver sky, with a background decoration in blue-green and bronze. The artist was Edward H. Fahey. Author's Collection.

tinually decried valentines because they were either useless or vulgar or both.

Among other points the leaflet proclaimed that the tradition of sending love tokens was not dead, but much alive, and described how in the United States the valentine trade was very flourishing.

Unanimously it was agreed to make all possible efforts to re-establish the custom of sending valentines, to make lavish displays in shop windows, to maintain high standards in quality and taste and to discourage the sale of vulgar and distasteful cards.

In the United States at this time the largest manufacturers were the McLoughlin Brothers of New York and the George C. Whitney Company of Worcester, Mass. Generally speaking, the style of valentine on sale in the U.S.A. in the 1880s and 1890s was still very much the same as those of earlier years. A coloured embossed background supported an elaborate layer or two of fancy paper on which would be a pretty motif, and each of the four corners would be ornamented with a small scrap, usually flowers or some similar decoration. Any

fancy open work or lace paper would always be shown up by being backed with coloured paper. By the 1900s there was a tendency for cards to be large; sometimes they were as much as eleven inches by eight in size. They carried a lot of heavy paper ornament by way of layers of gaily coloured scraps and fancy work, cleverly and artistically arranged to create a spectacular display of cherubs, hearts and flowers. Inside, on the third page a message or verse was printed within a decorated border. By far the most popular were the 'stand-ups' with honeycomb paper attachments, which were made in Germany. They were in all sizes and prices, costing from five cents to a dollar each, and depicted ships, carriages, automobiles, etc. The very large ones are scarce today, because being made of cheap pasteboard, they soon became broken and have failed to survive.

But, as the century drew to its close, it was evident how in England the giving and exchanging of cards on St. Valentine's Day was on the wane.

A journalist, writing his reminiscences of St. Valentine's Day in a London newspaper, compared the sta-

139. A popular Kate Greenaway study of the 1880s. On the reverse of the card is the message, "To my true and only Valentine". Author's Collection.

140. A charming little valentine, chromolithographed and published by De La Rue in the 1880s. Author's Collection.

140

142

141, 142. Two valentines by Louis Prang of Boston, 1882. Courtesy of the Hallmark Historical Collection.

143. Published by Raphael Tuck & Co., circa 1880, the fan measures over twelve inches across when opened out. Beautifully coloured in chromolithography. Author's Collection.

tioner's shop he was looking in, with its stock of æsthetic ornaments, new puzzles, somewhat indifferent fancy articles, and its valentines, to the village shop of his young days.

For the dear life of me in this year 1891, and on the 14th of February, I cannot make out what a valentine really is. Here are Berlin scent-bottles rich in indifferent gilt and badly fitting lids. These are valentines. Here are paper-weights, pads, and bottles; and these are valentines. No poetry, only parcel-post pine-wood boxes to hold them in, and yet they represent the sentiment of the most sentimental day of the whole year. It is really surprising, now in my middle age, when I look back upon my daisy days.

A valentine was a valentine then. Once more I am in the village shop and purchasing a lovely sheet of decorated letter paper edged with lace and with some ornate printing on it. A gentleman of that style of beauty which formerly decorated the lower class of hairdresser's shops

—a kind of *mélange* of Count D'Orsay, the late Lord Lytton, and certain members of the Royal family—a gentleman with sweet, small, curled moustache and side whiskers rather *à la Murat*, with a blue surtout coat of most voluminous folds, white waistcoat, nankeen trousers of the strongest gamboge, and shining boots—is walking up a winding path which leads to a distant village church. On the opposite side of the picture a lady with cannon curls, leg-of-mutton sleeves, and sandal shoes is lying on a sofa. The gentleman of the D'Orsay blue surtout is evidently the object of her affections and her dreams at the same time. He, the church spire, the winding path, and the blue surtout are surrounded by a series of imitation Dutch etchings—curved scratchings, evidently intended to represent clouds—the middle of the present century symbols of dreaming. At the top of the sheet a Cupid is superintending the general condition of a large, fleshly, very substantial, and far from ethereal heart. This was the valentine of the old days; and it was a valentine, as you could see by the touching inscription beneath :

114

My heart, my heart is always thine;
You are my only valentine.

The tucker edge of lacework developed in a broad breadth of tasteful Mechlin or Honiton. Glittering pieces of talc were gummed on to adorn a centre piece of cotton wool, pink ribbon, and stamped-out Cupids. The valentine itself was scented. On a satin disc, too, was printed a piece of tasteful verse. The print was good enough; as to the verse, perhaps I am not a judge. I can only say it was not very much above the average of the bonbon label, and did not do much in the way of rivalling the artistic advertisement of patent blacking, razor-strops, or scientific overalls. Still the valentine was more or less a valentine. There was poetry in it anyhow. Valentine was made to rhyme with sign, also with rime, and there was generally something about combine. If the valentine was further adorned with some bunches of Parmese violets, 7/6d. was the price that was charged. Still, I cannot help repeating, these things *were* valentines. But a change has come over the spirit of our dream. First of all was fastened to the valentine a pair of gloves. This, of course had a deep significance. It was an address to Phyllis to be rather froward than coy. Then came fans, then earrings, then scent-bottles, even side-combs and back-combs. The fact is, I am getting quite perplexed about the matter. What is a valentine? Why, only the other day I saw put up for sale as a valentine a case containing a pair of ebony-backed and silver-initialled hair-brushes. What possibly could be the connection between Messrs. Truefitt, say, and Cupid, or his patron St. Valentine?

Ugly valentines will always exist. Besides, it is the age of cheapness, and four colours will produce wonders, as any practical printer knows . . . and, as human nature is human nature, the ugly valentine will always flourish. Sold in conjunction with sweet-stuff, cheap walking-sticks, and ginger-beer, it can even hold its own against low-priced packets of cigarettes and lower-class weekly journals, at least for the time being—the happy time of St. Valentine. I have not sent any valentines this year . . . St. Valentine's gifts have dwindled into common-place perquisites.

Some interesting and amusing designs appeared in the modern style—art nouveau—during the 1890s. Some of these were drawn by Alfred Gray, an artist who specialised in black and white work. He designed envelopes with note-paper to match and produced a few cards as valentines. The two amusing cards illustrated in Plate 148 are typical of the æsthetic movement of this time and are reminiscent of Oscar Wilde.

144. A charming chromolithograph published by E. Nister, London. Author's Collection.

145. A charming chromolithograph published by Obpacher of New York in the 1880s. Courtesy of Hallmark Historical Collection.

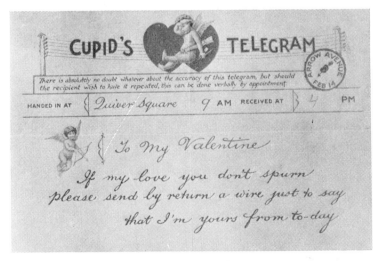

146. Published by E. P. Dutton & Co., New York (agents of Ernest Nister). Author's Collection.

Punch has amusingly summed up the attitude towards St. Valentine's Day in these verses which appeared in February, 1899:

A Lay of St. Valentine
(To an Old Tune)
Long ago in some far country
Dwelt an eminent divine
(When and where are no great matter),
And his name was Valentine.
But the Emperor was active
In the persecuting line,
Didn't like new-fangled notions,
Took the head off Valentine.
Oh, the sadness! Oh, the sadness! Oh, the madness,
Valentine!
For you lost your head for ever—dreadful sorry,
Valentine!

Later on they canonized him,
And did thoughtfully assign,
As a feast, the day he died on
To the good St. Valentine.
'Twas the day birds choose for mating,
And in loving pairs combine;
Followed suit the youths and maidens,
Called each other "Valentine".
Oh, the gladness! Oh, the gladness! Oh, the gladness,
Valentine!
You became a "joy for ever"—very nearly—
Valentine!

Then they sent each other pictures
Laced with fretted borders fine,
Hearts and arrows, gauzy cupids,
Tokens of St. Valentine.
I received and sent some dozens
Annually in days lang syne—
Now I should be quite contented,
Might I send *one* Valentine!
How irrational is Fashion! Foolish Fashion,
Valentine!
Now your day is done for ever—dreadful sorry,
Valentine!

147. Valentines of this sort, which folded flat, were made to pull out and to stand up. Usually made in Germany, they enjoyed a big sale in the U.S.A. about 1890-1905. Courtesy of Hallmark Historical Collection.

148, 149. Three cards reminiscent of the aesthetic movement in the 1890s. Two illustrated in colour lampoon the popular subject of the sunflower and lily; the other is a design on same theme by Alfred Gray. All from the Author's Collection.

A highly Poetic young man,
A love-in-an-attic young man,
A sunflower-and-lily, drive-the-girls-silly,
Ultra-romantic young man.

DECLINE AND REVIVAL

WITH the new century, about the only valentines which were being bought and used to any considerable extent were those printed as postcards. At this time the picture postcard was enjoying a great vogue; it was after all a fairly recent innovation, having come out in England as lately as September 1894, although it had been in use on the Continent for some twenty years or so.[1] This was because British postal regulations had made it difficult for publishers to print adequately a pictorial design on a government-issued postcard. The craze for collecting picture postcards at this time was one of the biggest collecting manias ever known, and everything that a postcard could show was depicted on it.

One of the pioneers in the picture postcard industry (for such it had become) was Messrs. Raphael Tuck and Sons Ltd., a firm which had always excelled in high-class design and production. They now published valentines in postcard form, beautifully printed and charming to look at. Other firms, too, especially those with German connections, turned to valentines on postcards, but the principal competition came from the numerous picture postcard manufacturers in Germany, whose similar high-class work was produced cheaply, and who catered to the tastes of all countries.

These German-made valentine postcards were exported not only to England but also to America where there was far more demand for them. In America, the custom of giving valentines had not lapsed as in Britain, and although not observed in the same way as it had been some ten or twenty years before, was none the less still being maintained.

The picture postcard valentine flourished in America, if the large numbers preserved in old postcard albums are any criterion, the heyday being the period 1907 to 1914, when the outbreak of war hampered the export of cards from Germany. For the most part, the cards are pleasantly designed, showing as a rule an abundance of plump cupids ethereally floating around hearts. Sometimes the cupids are embossed on a card and sometimes the hearts are of padded silk, giving the card an expensive appearance. Those designed by Ellen H. Clapsaddle and John Winsch are always wanted by collectors, although they are not always so attractive or so prettily designed as many of the German unsigned productions! Much sought after, too, are the cards printed in Leipzig by Meissner and Buch. These bear their title printed on the back as: 'St. Valentine's Souvenir Card.' They are

150. Printed in Germany, valentine postcards such as this enjoyed great popularity around 1905–1910. The heart is made of red padded silk. Author's Collection.

[1] In America, picture postcards had not been generally available until 1898, although, exceptionally, and by private enterprise, some had been printed since 1893; a few, in the form of greetings cards, had come out during the 1870s.

somewhat earlier than the others, having been published about 1897.

By World War I, in England, the valentine had almost become a thing of the past. In America, valentine makers continued to produce, but even so, the demand was not very great and the paper shortage made production difficult. A number of valentines of a patriotic theme came out when America joined the Allies, and helped to keep the custom alive. Some of these were published by the New York firm of Norcross, which had started business in 1914 and became one of the foremost publishers in America, responsible in later years for many beautiful valentines.

Following the First World War, St. Valentine's Day was still remembered in England; but only just! It is related that one day in 1925, Lady Jeanetta Tuck, when discussing with her husband, Sir Adolph Tuck, the Diamond Jubilee of the founding of the firm of Raphael Tuck, to take place the following year, suggested there could be no better way to celebrate such an event than by reviving the charming sentimental custom of sending valentines on the 14th of February. The idea was considered a good one and the next year the firm of Raphael Tuck re-established valentines. Once again lacy and decorative cards reminiscent of the past were seen in the shops and the public, especially the 'flappers', responded to the idea with enthusiasm. The revival made news, and many a newspaper devoted a column to it. *The Daily Telegraph* in its issue dated February 18, 1926, had this to say :

151. A delightful postcard designed by Frederick Spurgeon and published in England for leap year. It has the postmark February 13, 1912. Author's Collection.

An Amusing Revival

It is unfortunate that Feb. 14, that famous festival of birds and lovers, falls on a Sunday, since this year sees, after so long an interval, the revival of the valentine. Though it may be pleasant to receive these pretty conceits on the 13th or the 15th, it would be much more satisfactory if the postman could deliver them on the traditional date when his grandfather and great-grandfather were wont to deliver them.

Killed by facetious vulgarity and that baser imitation which is the insincerest form of flattery, the valentine has lain hidden away in that mysterious limbo of temporarily forgotten things, in company with the bustle, the shoulder shawl, and the tiny hinged parasol. It has just made a tentative reappearance in a vastly changed world. Has it returned merely on that wave of fashion which has brought back into favour so many Victorian notions not so long ago held in artistic horror? Now that the tinkling glass chandelier is prized, as well as black trays embellished with the convolvulus and the peony, painted china door-plates, wax flowers, and china figures, and the embroidered footstool and firescreen, the valentine may well become a fashionable toy... The arbiters of fashion have tried hard to banish femininity from women's clothes, hairdressing, and speech, but it keeps breaking out in all sorts of unexpected places. As hats, for instance, become smaller and plainer slippers grow more elaborate and jewelled; the slim figure as straight as a boy's is the present-day ideal, yet lipsticks and powder are in universal use. The damsel with an Eton crop still uses toilet preparations with ultra-feminine names such as 'Beauty of the Desert' or 'Queen of the Harem'. So perhaps the modern girl is wearying of being called 'old bean,' and is developing a craving for the sweet and satisfying language of the romantics.

119

152. Printed in delicate shades of red, blue and green on a parchment-like paper, and fringed with real lace. The fan opens to disclose a message:
"Every time you look at me, My heart goes pitter-patter
But for heaven's sake Don't look that way Unless I really matter."
English, dated 1937. Author's Collection.

153. An American valentine of World War I, about 1918. Courtesy of the Norcross Collection, New York.

The valentines of to-day are artistically designed and well printed, resembling closely the more expensive type of Christmas card; but I cannot pretend that those I have seen rival in charm the old-fashioned kind preserved in our grandmothers' albums. The designers of the valentines of the 'sixties and 'seventies understood that in the matter of sentiment there must be not only a lavish prodigality at the finish, but a deliberate and delicate approach. . . .

An extension of the usual valentine might be suggested in this age of changed conditions and platonic relationships, and that is the designing of two different types of card—one the orthodox, straightforward variety for the use of golden lads and lassies, and the other more sober and restrained, to express that calmer affection and friendship between men and women which has yet a delicate thread of sentiment running through it. Now that the charming art of letter-writing is dead such a valentine, if done with tact, might be a graceful and a welcome compromise.

No such revival took place in America—for none was needed. The custom persisted, largely helped by the schools, which were instrumental in no small way in keeping alive the memory of the saint. Children would bring a valentine to teacher, and in this way many a school-marm's popularity was gauged! In America, too, the age-old custom of 'drawing' for one's valentine was kept up in many schools by the pupils bringing their valentines to be placed in a box, and then being given out. This custom is known by the author to have been observed as recently as ten years ago.

It was in 1910 also that the firm of Hallmark was established in Kansas City, Missouri. Starting in a small way as Hall Brothers, this firm probably has done more than any other to foster the popularity and use of valentines, and is today beyond doubt the largest concern of its kind in the world.

The revival in England persisted, and people were again accustomed to the exchange of valentine cards. The little fan shown in Plate 152 might be considered above general standard. Edged with real lace, and dated in 1937, it is made of a vellum-like paper, and opens to disclose the message:

> Everytime you look at me
> My heart goes pitter-patter
> But for heaven's sake
> Don't look that way
> Unless I really matter.

154. A Post Office Greetings Telegram for St. Valentine's Day, 1938. Author's Collection.

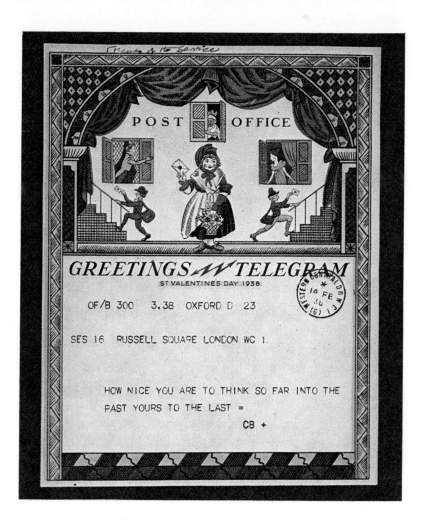

The British Post Office, too, helped by issuing very attractive St. Valentine's Day greetings telegrams, brightly coloured and suitably decorated. These were very popular, and, delivered in a neat golden envelope, gave great pleasure. The first one to appear for St. Valentine's Day was in 1936, designed by Rex Whistler.

Since the end of World War II, Saint Valentine is again holding his own. Each year the shops display his tokens, the windows and shelves resplendent and gay with brightly decorated valentines. Generally, the quality and taste is good. Humorous ones are popular, just as they have always been, but there are not many which could be termed objectionable.

More interesting is the steady revival of the observance of St. Valentine's Day in certain other European countries. The presence of American servicemen in Germany created a great demand for valentines, and this stimulated interest among the native population. Today, in several cities in Germany, it has become customary for a young man to present his loved one with a bunch of flowers on February 14. Likewise in Vienna and in other parts of Austria this custom is becoming general. In Spain, too, courting couples now exchange gifts and husbands send flowers to their wives.

In Italy, it has been the custom in the city of Turin for young people to announce their engagement on the 14th of February, and for a short while before Saint Valentine's Day, the *confiserie* shops are gay with daintily beribboned little china containers in the form of baskets and cups, filled with bon-bons of all sorts. This custom is gradually spreading to other cities in Italy.

St. Valentine's Day is the one Saint's Day in our calendar which does not depend on the Church for its celebration and, although its observance sometimes wanes, it seems fairly certain after all these years that the Saint's Day will never be completely overlooked, but will continue to be remembered regularly in February each year "when every fowl cometh to chose his make".

APPENDIX I

SAINT VALENTINE

It is not known for certain which Saint Valentine is being honoured as the Patron Saint of Lovers on the 14th of February, because history records two saints of this name, both martyred at about the same time and both buried on the Flaminian Way, outside the Porta del Popolo of Rome.

During the Victorian era, when the giving of valentines was so popular, the story of the saint was often written-up in the form of articles which appeared fairly regularly as the Saint's Day came round. Many of the writers more or less copied what had already been written before, but some, more serious, such as Professor John W. Hales, endeavoured to trace the origins and to give a more studious account. Professor Hales wrote an extremely interesting and learned article in the February 1882 number of *The Antiquary*. But it is thanks to Alban Butler, an eighteenth-century historian, who wrote an account of the lives of the saints, that the description and manner of the saint's martyrdom has been recorded in the way we know. Some writers refer to Valentine as a Roman priest, and others to Bishop Valentine.

According to general belief, both the priest and the Bishop, who can be identified as the Bishop of Terni, a small town about 80 miles from Rome, were martyred in the same way and on the same day, the year varying between A.D. 270 and 273. This is repeated in the *Encyclopedia Britannica* which adds, "that the Passion of the priest Valentine is part of the legend of SS. Marius and Martha and their companions; that of the latter has no better historical foundation; so that no argument can be drawn from either account to establish the difference of the two saints. . . ." The account concludes by saying that *The Martyrologium Hieronymianum* mentions only one Valentinus: *Interamnae Miliario LXIIII via Flaminia natale Valentini*.

In a recent enquiry of the Comissione per l'Archeologia Cristiana in Rome, reference was made to the *Enciclopedia Cristiana* where it is stated that Saint Valentine was born in Terni, and is called a Roman martyr because in the year 273 he was executed in Rome, and because at that time Terni, which is within 100 miles of Rome, was under Roman jurisdiction. This therefore might be the reason for the confusion, the Bishop of Terni being referred to as a Roman Bishop. The Bishop of Terni is venerated at Terni, where, within a small Basilica to his memory, is an altar containing his relics. In the small ancient church of St. Praxedes in Rome is a glass-fronted wooden box which contains some of the bones of St. Valentine, together with those of St. Zenone. There can be little doubt that the Bishop of Terni and the Roman priest are one and the same.

From an unknown source comes the story that the Emperor Claudius issued a decree forbidding people to marry, because marriage kept men at home and the Emperor wanted all men to be soldiers and to fight for Rome. The good Valentine ignored this decree and invited young lovers to come to him in secret to be united with the blessing of the Church. Their secret marriages were discovered and the Emperor commanded Valentine to be thrown into prison and later executed. Another legend connected with the saint relates that whilst in prison awaiting his execution, he attempted to restore the sight of the keeper's blind daughter, whom he had befriended. ". . . From that time the Girl became enamoured of him, nor did he treat her Affection with Contempt. But after a long imprisonment he was ordered for Publick Execution on the 14th of February. While in Prison being deprived of Books, he used to amuse himself with cutting curious Devices in Paper, on one of which he wrote some pious Exhortations and Assurances of Love, and sent to the Keeper's Daughter the Morning of Execution; and being concluded in the Words, 'Your Valentine' there is great reason for supposing that to be the origin of the present Custom."

This little story is quoted from *Kemmish's Annual* for 1797, and is reputed to come from "a very old book", but a moment's reflection is sufficient to suggest this pretty little anecdote to be only fiction. It is perhaps unfortunate that the story is perpetuated by being related to schoolchildren and is sometimes quoted by greetings cards manufacturers. In this way, fiction and legend can so often be represented as fact.

APPENDIX II

LOVE-TOKENS

For centuries gloves have been a popular form of present to give to one's Valentine on the 14th of February, the custom going back at least to the 16th century. Expensive gifts in the form of jewellery were very usual among the wealthier and more exalted; no doubt ordinary folk gave gifts of jewels and trinkets, too, but accounts and records of those in a more humble station of life have not been handed down in the same way.

From the diary of Samuel Pepys we learn that not only gloves, but garters too were commonly given to one's Valentine, and we also hear of little Will Mercer making a prettily ornamented card with a name designed on it.

An interesting love-token in a traditional design is that shown in Plate 157; the date has been given as about 1700 by the Victoria and Albert Museum. The heart, which measures about an inch and a half across is covered with a rich brocade in red and white on one side, and entirely in red on the other. The little metal arrow which pierces it is tipped with chicken's feathers.

Sailors thought fondly of their sweethearts whilst away on their long voyages, and beguiled the time by carving or scratching designs on pieces of tusk or bone. These drawings, known as scrimshaw work, are sometimes most attractively done. Often they show a ship, or a scene at sea, and carry loving and affectionate messages. Common gifts of this kind were stay busks which were stiffeners for corsets. The stay busk, shown in Plate 155, is carved out of a hard wood; the upper end is adorned by a heart, whilst in the lower part can be seen the traditional pair of doves. The portrait in the middle might well be that of the giver. On the other side is carved the date, 1786, together with the lady's name,

Sarah Burgin. An even more elaborate reminder of this sort of token is the busk carved from a sperm whale's jaw having the lines:

Accept dear girl, this busk from me
Carved by my humble hand
I took it from a sperm whale's jaw
One thousand miles from land.
In many a gale Had been the whale
In which this bone did rest.
His time is past, His bone at last
Must now support thy breast.

Love-tokens, too, were commonly given by way of little ivory or bone bobbins used for making lace. Love messages delicately pricked in along the sides would say "The gift is small but love is all", or "My love for thee no one can tell", and other simple expressions of this sort.

Another kind of love-token mostly favoured in country districts was the knitting sheath, which was a piece of wood about 9 inches long, decoratively carved to the best of the giver's ability. Having a hole at one end, it was fashioned in such a way, that, when tucked into a waist belt, the wearer would have her right hand free.

In the latter part of the 18th century it would be general for a young woman to give her sweetheart a small circular piece of material of silk or satin, the size of a watch, on which she had embroidered her name, with the date and an expression of affection such as: 'Remember Me', or her initials along with those of her lover enclosed in a heart. These were used instead of the ordinary watch papers which, embellished with fine engraving and the name of the watchmaker, were commonly put inside the enveloping metal case of a watch, and served to keep the dust out of the works.

Forerunners of the pictorial valentine as we know it today, were the hand-made True-Love Knots, the puzzle purses, and other decorative handwritten letters with

155. A stay busk carved out of wood. Sailors would carve these out of bone or some foreign wood as a gift for a sweetheart.

156. Love Token or Valentine: a Liverpool Jug, bearing a usual valentine design with 'Endless Knot of Love' motif. Courtesy of Carroll Alton Means, Connecticut.

sets of verses and sentimental messages of love. Along with these, in the early years of the 19th century and right up to the 1850s, little containers and comfit boxes of Bilston or Battersea ware were suitably inscribed with a well-chosen sentiment.

Mugs, cups, jugs and dishes of Sunderland ware made useful valentines. The one shown in Plate 156 is a handsome jug of Liverpool ware decorated like a valentine; the Endless Knot of Love is on one side, and a picture on the other.

A most delightful love-token which was shown to the author is a neatly bound little volume of love poems; the edges of the pages are gilded, but fore-edged, so that by slightly fanning out the pages a coloured design is revealed with the words: "To My Valentine".

It follows, of course, that love tokens were given on any occasion and at any time, and not only on the 14th of February, although St. Valentine's Day was often favoured.

The writer of the newspaper article quoted on page 114 expressed himself bewildered at the sight of such things as scent bottles, paper weights and other fancy articles being called valentines, and he pined for the lovely lace-edged pictorial valentine with verses, such as he remembered as a young man. He was obviously not aware that a valentine does not need to be a pretty picture with verses, and for centuries past a gift to one's sweetheart in the form of gloves, garters, jewellery—anything in fact given with love—was accepted by way of a valentine gift.

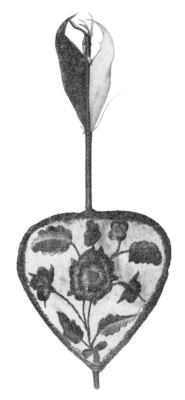

157. A brocaded heart pierced by a feather – a love-token of about 1700. Courtesy of P. Withers, Reading.

158. Embroidered on fine gauze backed with paper, a late eighteenth-century watch paper. Author's Collection.

APPENDIX III

LACE PAPER MAKING

It has long been wondered how the beautiful lace paper which embellished valentines was made. Embossed paper and card had been commonly used since the middle of the 18th century and can be found ornamenting visiting cards which were often made with a decorated embossed edge. Examples are known, too, having a certain amount of open work, but being of stiff paper or card, cannot be called lace-work, although the semblance is there.

By the end of the 18th century many of the German and Viennese greetings cards were beautifully embossed with almost cameo-like effect. Perforated paper was also now being made, and in a description written by one of the old-time valentine manufacturers of the 1840s, it is said that the French were making a form of lace paper in the early part of the century. This was writing paper of the quarto size with a decorated border perforated with pin-pricked holes of varying sizes.

A much earlier attempt would seem to be the lace work which shows on the valentine published in London in 1797, illustrated in Plate 29, as well as the better example on a valentine dated 1802, shown in Plate 32.

In notes made by Jonathan King, it is said that Joseph Addenbrooke, whilst in the employ of Dobbs, the fancy stationers and embossers, happened on the process of making lace paper quite by chance, sometime in the 1830s. A sheet of paper was caught on the male die as it was being removed from the ball press. A file brushed over it and the thinned paper on the high points disappeared. Addenbrooke improved on his discovery. He made lace dies with a net background, put the paper in three sheets at a time, laying the sheets on the male half of the die, and scraped off the weakened high points with a few strokes of a file. The result was lace paper.

Addenbrooke then left the firm of Dobbs and opened up on his own, at 101 Hatton Garden, London, but he didn't keep his secret to himself, for very soon lace paper was being made by all the others in the trade.

It will be of interest to many to know that a pioneer who experimented in the development and manufacture of lace paper was Sir Henry Bessemer. In his autobiography,[1] he describes how, in 1833, after a certain amount of practice he "produced a great many beautiful dies, from which thousands of fine stamp impressions were made. I erected a powerful 'Fly Press' for stamping impressions from the dies and thus achieved what was in reality my first commercial work. . . ." He relates how he produced dies for embossing on card and on leather and how he designed a revenue stamp which would be impossible to forge. For this he turned his attention to the invention of a steel die which made perforations and submitted the design of his stamp to the Stamp Office. This was a circular stamp about $2\frac{1}{2}$ inches in diameter, having the device of a garter and shield, and the value *Five Pounds*, the space between the garter and shield being filled with network in imitation of lace. "The die was made of steel and pierced the parchment (on which the stamp was printed) with more than four hundred holes, each one of the necessary form to produce its special portion of the design. Since that period, perforated paper has been largely employed for valentines and other ornamental purposes, but was previously unknown. . . ." However, for a variety of reasons, his design was turned down. Another stamp, this time designed for postage, with an embossed lace-work effect was actually considered in 1839. When the plan for a uniform penny post was being discussed, the Treasury invited members of the public, particularly artists and scientists to submit proposals for postage stamps to serve on letters by way of prepayment, having a special regard to convenience and security against forgery. A money prize was offered, but none of the entries sent in was considered suitable, although four of the competitors were given an award for merit. One of these was Charles Whiting, a well-known embosser (*see* page 133) and another was Benjamin Cheverton of Camden Town. His essay was a circular embossed stamp, about half an inch in diameter, with the Royal Monogram, VR, surmounted by a crown, and the words POST OFFICE below. Finely and delicately made, its lace-like appearance resembled a miniature doily.

In *All The Year Round*, a weekly journal edited by Charles Dickens, a very informative article describing a visit to a valentine manufactory, where lace-paper making was done, appeared in the issue for February 20,

[1] *Sir Henry Bessemer, F.R.S. An autobiography*, published by *Engineering*, London, 1905

1864. The name and address of this maufacturer is only thinly disguised and can easily be seen to be that of Joseph Mansell, one of the best known, and famous for the high quality of his work. Under the title, *Cupid's Manufactory*, the article explains at length the making of a lace-paper valentine from start to finish :

Cupid's Manufactory

The name and address of the eminent manufacturing firm of Cupid and Co. are not to be found in the Post-office Directory. I know this because I have searched the magnum opus through all its divisions without being able to discover them. Nevertheless, the firm has not only a name but a local habitation; and I have visited the habitation, been over the works, and know all about the concern. I have long aspired to possess this knowledge. Years past, when, long before the advent of the month which is popularly supposed to usher in the mating season of both birds and men, I have noticed the windows of small booksellers and stationers break out into a pictorial rash in anticipation of the Feast of St. Valentine, I have been in the habit of wondering how and where the outbreak originated. . . .

. . . from information I received, I proceeded there, and found Cupid and Company actively engaged in their business, on extensive premises situated in Love-lane, number thirty-five. Perhaps you are unacquainted with Love-lane : may never have heard of it before. Well,—no matter; if you should ever go there, you will find it remarkably like Red Lion-square. . . . The outside of Cupid's manufactory is perhaps a little disenchanting to the visitor, who has been drawing fancy pictures of it in his mind coming along. If you expect wreaths and festoons, you will be disappointed; if you look for cornucopias, you will not find them; if you have called up a vision of Cupid swinging on a rope of roses over the doorway, you will not realise that vision. You find simply a plain brick house, bearing no other emblem of the trade carried on within than a pair of iron extinguishers on each side of the doorway, in which, by a considerable stretch of the imagination, you may conceive the torch of Hymen to have been occasionally quenched, at a period prior to the introduction of gas. Neither the red rose, nor the blue violet, nor the sweet carnation, embowers the windows; these being wholly unadorned, rather dingy, and provided each with a wire blind, on which are painted, in the severest prose, the words 'Cupid and Co., Manufacturers'.

Entering that mundane doorway, and wiping my feet on that cocoa-nut mat, of the earth earthy, I could not conceive the realm of sublimated fancy which lay beyond. . . . I was not, however, inducted to the mysteries too suddenly. A Youth, in all the elegance of turned-up shirt-sleeves, came and took my card, and I had to wait in the counting-house—Cupid's counting-house! until he returned, which he eventually did, quite at his leisure, whistling what at first hearing appeared to be Love's Young Dream, but which I presently recognised as a melody less in harmony with the genius loci—namely, The Whole Hog or None. Would I step this way? I did so with a nervous hesitation natural to the novelty of my position, and next moment found myself confronted with a remarkably good-looking little gentleman, who acknowledged, in answer to my polite insinuation in that direction, that he was Cupid. I don't know that I was quite prepared for the personal appearance he presented. It had never occurred to me to picture the God of Love, even in his manufacturing capacity, otherwise than in a full suit of wings and with a bow and arrow. But here he stood before me in a black frock-coat and a pair of—possibly Sydenham—trousers. . . . Cupid received me with a courtesy which was most flattering, considering that I had come there, a stranger, boldly preferring a request to be shown over his establishment, and initiated into the mysteries of his craft. He was ready to show me all without reserve, and, leading the way, he introduced me at once into the press-room.

It was like a chamber in the Mint. The knobbed arms of five or six fly-presses were swinging about so near each other that it seemed impossible to steer through them without being dashed to pieces. I did not try. The presses were stopped, and I was shown how a plain sheet of paper was prepared for a lace-edged valentine. Every one is familiar with the process of die-stamping, so this part of the operation will not require minute description. The paper is laid upon the matrice, the arms of the press are swung round and the die descends, embossing the paper by one pressure. But the dies here are no ordinary dies, and the process is yet far from complete. Each die consists of a heavy square block of iron enclosed with the matrice in a metal box, which is furnished with two handles like the legs of a pair of tongs, for the convenience of the operator. The design, after being drawn upon the surface of the iron, is hammered into it by means of steel punches. The iron of the die, of course, is softer—or rather I should say less hard—than the material of the punch; but when the design is completed the die is hardened by the usual process of tempering. A great number and variety of punches are required to execute a design. For example, in an embossed border every little hexagon, every dot, and every flower, requires a separate punch. The execution of a design, therefore, is a tedious and expensive process. There are, perhaps, a hundred different dies about the room, and some of them have cost nearly twenty pounds. The matrices are made of mill-board, and, ranged on shelves round the walls, look like a library of well-thumbed dog-eared books. I am now standing aside, and the fly-presses are in full swing embossing two or three sheets of paper each per minute. Some of these sheets are plain; others contain a picture in the centre, as, for example, . . . a lady and gentleman, who, with the pathway and the church, have already been printed on the paper by the familiar process of lithography. They are now receiving embossed borders. The next process is to convert these borders into paper lace, with all the interstices proper to the particular kind which the design represents. The dies are removed from the presses, and with the embossed sheets handed over to a distinct set of workmen in another room. These workmen, who practise this branch of the manufacture solely and exclusively, lay the embossed paper neatly on the die, adjusting it exactly by means of regulating pins at the corners, and then with flat iron tools covered with fine sand-paper, rub off the projecting bosses on the paper. This process is very neatly and rapidly performed, and a strip of Valenciennes or Mechlin starts out under the tool at every rub. In this room a dozen workmen do nothing else all day long but use the sand-paper file. It is a very magical way of making lace, and the operation seems easy, but it is not so easy as it seems. It requires great nicety of touch not to tear the paper. One of the pressmen down stairs who essayed to complete the process for my benefit, signally failed with the sand-paper file, and tore what might have been a gorgeous messenger of love, all to tatters.

Let us follow our valentine step by step from its cradle to—I will not say its grave, but to that neat white box in which it is packed, with others of its kind, to be sent out to the trade. Let us say that we begin with the sheet of paper bearing the plain, unadorned presentment of the lady and gentleman lovingly wending their way towards the sacred fane. We have seen them encompassed by an embossed border; we have seen that border magically transformed into lace. But still, with all this, the valentine remains in the penny plain condition. Now, however, it passes into the twopence coloured department—a long room, containing some twenty neat-handed nymphs seated at a bench, each with a little pot of liquid watercolour at her elbow. Valentine comes into the hand of nymph number one. Nymph lays it flat before her, and places over its surface a perforated sheet of cardboard, the perforations in which correspond exactly with, say the pathway. The brush is dipped in the pot of pale brown and daubed over the perforations. Behold the pale brown

159. A devotional valentine of the mid-eighteenth century on white vellum. This particularly fine example is hand made and is about eight by six inches in size. The exquisite scissors and knife work closely resembles the finest lace paper of a century later. The picture of Saint Thérèse holding the sacred heart in her hand is painted in gouache, as are also the little flowers that surround it. The similarity of these to the small coloured floral scraps so commonly used on Victorian valentines is striking. Author's Collection.

pathway! The valentine passes to nymph number two, who uses another stencil plate of cardboard, and daubs in the salmon-covered church. Number three in the same manner dashes in the gentleman's blue coat, number four his yellow waistcoat, number five his lilac continuations, number six the lady's green mantle, number seven the lady's pink bonnet, while it probably remains for other nymphs to clothe the fields with verdure, and indicate the smiling morn by tipping the hills with gold. Thus a highly-coloured valentine passes through at least half a dozen hands in the process of colouring, or pooning as it is technically called. The pooning cards, perforated with all sorts of irregular holes, and daubed with various colours, have a very odd appearance, lying together in a heap on a bench. A stranger to these mysteries could not possibly guess the use of such queer things. He would probably arrive at the conclusion that they were the efforts, not of methodical genius, but of most unmethodical madness.

When our valentine has passed through this room, it is, for all ordinary purposes, complete, and, with a lace border and highly-coloured illustration, may be sold at prices varying from sixpence to half-a-crown; but if it aspire to value itself at five shillings or half a guinea, it must yield to further adornment in another department. Again, a long room occupied by nymphs, each one having at her elbow a pot, not of colour this time, but of glue. Strewed before each girl in apparent confusion, but really in regularly-assorted heaps, lie hearts and darts and doves and bows and arrows, and rose-buds and true lovers' knots, and torches of Hymen, and every variety of emblem appertaining to love and matrimony. These ornaments are cut out of every kind of material by means of punches. Some are paper, some are silk and velvet, some tinsel and gold-leaf. The business of the girls here is to stick these ornaments upon the valentines, so as perhaps to enclose the picture in a posie of flowers and emblems. Our lady and gentleman are now under treatment. You will observe that there is an unadorned space between the border and the picture. This is about to be filled up, and the basis of the operation is a series of paper springs. Cupid, who is in close attendance, explaining everything in the most obliging manner, says to the nymph, "Show the gentleman how you make paper springs." It is done in a moment. A strip of writing-paper is doubled lengthways alternately backwards and forwards three times— in the form of a pipe-light—and then cut into lengths of about half an inch. The lower ends of these springs are fastened to the valentine with glue, and then upon the upper surfaces are fixed strips of plain flat paper. Upon these strips the nymph, according to a design which lies before her, arranges flowers and love-knots and all kinds of devices. Immediately over the church she glues on a gilt Cupid; at the corners she places birds'-nests with eggs; down the sides, festoons of flowers, relieved here and there with united hearts and crossed darts and lyres and flying doves. This decoration forms a pretty bas-relief frame to the picture, and the paper springs which support it permit the frame to be pressed flat for the convenience of packing. Each of the girls in this department is at work upon a different design, some of which are exceedingly pretty and tasteful. Some, too, are very expensive. Here, for example, is one containing in the centre a really well-executed picture, in the ivory miniature style, of Cupid, surrounded by a rich ornamental border studded with pearls. The price of this elegant article enclosed in an enamelled box neatly tied up with white satin ribbon is two guineas. I am naturally curious to know if many of these are sold. The answer to my query is, "A good many." I am informed, however, that the most expensive chiefly go to the colonies. I could imagine a gold-digger buying this valentine with the pearls, and paying for it with a nugget. It seems very absurd to give two guineas for a valentine, but the one under notice really appears to be worth the money. It is a most elaborate affair, and, as a piece of delicate workman and workwomanship, *looks* to be better worth the price than many fancy articles of more intrinsic value which we see in the windows of the jewellers. The brightly-coloured varnished flowers that are used in this department have hitherto been made almost exclusively in Germany, but Cupid informs me, with great satisfaction, that he will shortly be in a position to compete with the Germans on their own ground, and dispense with foreign aid altogether.

Our lady and gentleman are now proceeding to church under every imaginable circumstance of glory. Cupid keeps watch over them with more than a cherub's personality, doves flutter round them, flowers bloom at their feet, while the air is laden with a rich perfume, emanating, I am bound to state, from a pinch of Jockey Club artfully inserted in a piece of cotton wool, and stowed away under the exalted seat of Cupid. Still our lady and gentleman have to pass through another ordeal. They must step into the next room and be examined. Nymphs again are the examiners, and there are six of them. They sit here permanently, as a committee of taste. If there be anything wrong, a dove flying with its feet in the air, a Cupid standing on his head, or a rose violating the laws of nature by growing downward, the lady and gentleman are sent back to have their glorious surroundings put to rights; if not, they receive the imprimatur of approval, and are placed in cardboard boxes to be delivered to the trade.

In following the progress of our valentine from the embossing-room to the finishing department, we have passed in review about sixty hands, nearly forty of these being girls, the rest men and boys. In all the departments the work struck me as being of a healthy and cheerful kind. The rooms are well lighted and airy, and the girls exhibit none of the languor and weariness which are painfully apparent in the workrooms of the milliner and dressmaker. They are very neatly dressed, and some of them are very pretty, and these appearances, together with a briskness of manner and a cheerfulness of expression, convinced me that if the Song of the Valentine were written, it would form a happy contrast to the Song of the Shirt. The girls work from eight o'clock in the morning till seven o'clock at night, with intervals for dinner and tea, and their wages range from five to fifteen shillings a week, the average being ten for the skilled hands, and five for young beginners—mere children, who certainly could not earn as much money at anything else. Although there are slack and busy seasons in this trade, as in every other, the employment is pretty regular all the year round. At this moment artists and die-sinkers are at work for next year. About June or July their designs will be finished, and copies struck off for the travellers who go out with their pattern-books, as early as August. And there are articles besides valentines made here: articles which come in at unpoetical seasons, to keep the machinery of the establishment in full play. . . .

. . . Two of the questions which I often put to myself in the days when I was wholly ignorant of the great valentine economy yet remain unanswered. Who draws the pictures? Who writes the poetry? For a practical elucidation of this mystery we very properly and fitly go up-stairs to the higher regions of the establishment. In a well-lighted room, exclusively devoted to art, we find six draughtsmen transferring their designs to stone. The designs are highly finished and elaborately coloured, and some of them are really beautiful. They don't look so well when they are printed, for much the same reason that a wood-engraving rarely comes up to the original drawing. They are spoilt by the heavy-handed process of colouring, as the drawing on wood is often marred by the engraver. There are no middle tints. It goes, if you will excuse the popular phrase, the whole hog or none. Bright blue or nothing, blood red and no surrender! Looking, however, at some of the drawings, I can detect no fault in them. I have seen worse things on the stairs of the Royal Academy. But these designs are intended for the superior order of valentines. The common kinds and the comic kinds are drawn out of doors. Nothing coarse or vulgar is issued from this establishment, and the common specimens are only common, in so far as the paper is inferior and the drawing is dashed in with more regard to effect than finish. The subjects of some of the comic valentines are copied from drawings in Punch and his humorous contemporaries, but the great majority of them are original, and deal mainly with the passing follies and fashions of the day—crinoline, the Dundreary whiskers, the jacket coat, the spoon bonnet, and so forth. The regular comic artist of the establishment—a very clever fellow, by the way—does not work on the premises: . . . I understand that he is a highly prosperous person, that he drives up to the door in a Hansom cab, and is very sharp and short with the head of the firm. The poet, too, works out; but it was my happiness to meet him on the door-step on taking my leave. I am bound to say that he looked like a poet. He had raven ringlets, wore a cloak with a velvet collar, and had a fine phrensy in his eye. I caught it just as it was rolling, and I said to myself, "Nascitur, non fit." What does he sing of our lady and gentleman church-ward-bound along the pale brown pathway?

> The path before me gladly would I trace,
> With one who's dearest to my constant heart,
> To yonder church, the holy sacred place,
> Where I my vows of Love would fain impart;
> And in sweet wedlock's bonds unite with thee,
> Oh, then, how blest my life would ever be!

And there is that rather sporting-looking young man, in the green waistcoat and the pink necktie, grasping by the hand the generally blue maiden in the gipsy hat under the cliffs—apparently of Dover—who thus pours forth his soul:

> Ne'er doubt, fair maid, the vows I make,
> A constant heart no time can shake;
> Rather than cause it e'er to wander,
> Time, the true heart, makes grow fonder.

Our poet is evidently of a serious turn, and given to the sentimental and the pathetic; finds it difficult to screw himself down to the low level of the comic. There is quite a touch of the pastoral style in the opening line of his satire upon the lady in the spoon bonnet:

> Tell me, gentle lady fair,
> Why such ugly things you wear.
> Surely all your wits are fled,
> A spoon to carry on your head.

He is almost didactic in his severity upon the gentleman with the scrubbing-brush beard, who is admiring himself in the looking-glass:

> Looking at thyself within the glass,
> You appear lost in admiration;
> You deceive yourself, and think, alas!
> You are a wonder of creation.

If it be alleged that the poet-laureate of Love is somewhat halt, it must be remembered that Love himself is blind. I have not heard that a butt of sherris sack forms part of the reward of Cupid's laureate; but I believe his verses are estimated as being worth twopence a line, which is, at any rate, a penny over the conventionally standard price of prose. At this price, the poem just quoted would come to eightpence. But the great difficulty in dealing with the valentine poet is to make him comprehend that brevity is not only the soul of wit, but the essence of economy. His efforts are very frequently vain, owing to his strong disposition to spin the subject out to twelve lines, and make an even shilling of it. There are many pounds of poetry up-stairs that would have been declined with thanks had they not been furnished by contract. . . .

Cupid informs me that, in the height of his season, he turns out two hundred and fifty pounds' worth of valentines a week, and at these times he pays about a hundred and sixty pounds a week in wages. That his business is yearly on the increase is proved by the annual report of the Postmaster-General, which shows that, while the number of valentines which passed through the London office in 1862 was four hundred and thirty thousand, in 1863 it was upwards of four hundred and fifty thousand. The iron of our age has not entered the national soul so deeply, after all.

160. Jonathan King in his workroom. Courtesy of Carroll Alton Means, Connecticut.

APPENDIX IV

JONATHAN KING —
COLLECTOR PAR EXCELLENCE
by Carroll Alton Means

When Gleeson White, writer on art subjects and editor of *The Studio* (London) decided in 1894 that the Christmas card, then in its third decade of commercial production, deserved public notice, he sought facts from the publishers, but was referred to Jonathan King of Islington, described as the "Master of all Christmas card collectors—owner of a collection which aimed at possessing a copy of every single design". White discovered that King had followed the subject from inside knowledge, more closely perhaps, than any other living person. His collection, contained in 700 volumes, weighing, collectively, between six and seven tons, included about 163,000 varieties, and although not exhaustive offered what was "practically a completely illustrated history of the many years between 1862 and 1894". In his valued publication, "Christmas Cards and their

Chief Designers", issued as an extra number of *The Studio* for Christmas, 1894, White described Jonathan King as "the collector *par excellence*".

In his initial search for information, Mr. White had found the British Museum of little help, possessing a mere handful of greeting card items. He therefore encouraged King to go on with his collecting in the hope that public interest would ultimately influence the museum authorities to correct the deficiency by acquiring this great collection. He observed, "If space can be found for complete sets of railway time tables and other records of similar intrinsic value, it would be regrettable did a collection of Christmas cards fail to obtain a place".

Strongly encouraged, Jonathan King continued collecting, buying entire establishments to get sample books and other material which he wanted. Active concerns sent him their latest sample books and in return received valuable advice on such subjects as infringement. By 1911, King's collection had increased to 1,500 volumes, including 250 devoted exclusively to valentines. By his own estimate he felt that he had close to a million greeting cards and about 30,000 valentines. To this should be added great quantities of supplementary material such as drawings, original verses, wood-blocks, lace-paper dies, samples of paper and envelopes, ornaments, etc. The collection filled four rooms with shelves, specially built for the purpose, and overflowed on to stairways and into living quarters. Its weight was now close to fifteen tons and the problem of preservation proportionately great.

Jonathan King's entire working life was devoted to the business of valentines and greeting cards. He was born on October 28, 1836, the son of another Jonathan and his wife, Clarissa Honeysett. The elder Jonathan served his apprenticeship as a stationer under his uncle, Charles King. In 1845 he opened a small establishment at 45 Chapel Street, Somerstown, dealing in juvenile plays and valentines as supplements to the daily business of newspapers and tobacco. Mrs. King designed the first lace-paper valentines and supervised their production in wholesale quantities. In 1848 Jonathan King the son, aged 12, started working for his father. The business prospered and in 1852 it was moved to larger quarters at 56 (later 43) Seymour Street, Euston Square. Here, in 1869, the elder Jonathan King died.

Our Jonathan had helped expand the business by opening up a shop at 22 Stevenson Terrace (afterwards 295 Caledonian Road) to which he took his bride, Emily Elizabeth Ashford, in 1861. She ran the store at this address while Jonathan served as traveller for his father. After the father's death, the combined businesses were moved in 1871 to a new location at 302 and 304 Essex Road, Islington. Here double-houses (called Barozza villas) were occupied by the growing family. A factory was erected in the front garden with three one-storey stores fronting in Essex Road. The corner store (302) was the retail store, known as the "Fancy Valentine Shop", which was run under the name of Mrs. King (E. E. King). This responsibility passed to the eldest daughter, Ellen Rose King, when the mother became involved with the younger members of her large family (fifteen children, of whom thirteen survived childhood). Curiously, the fourteenth child was named Sydney Valentine King, in honour of his mother's birthplace (Sydney, Australia) and St. Valentine's Day (the 14th of February).

Jonathan King was a successful business man and an exacting father. He ruled his family according to fixed rules which required each child to assume certain definite responsibilities. Suffering from his own lack of formal education, he saw to it that his children were well provided for. This superior education was largely responsible for the business decline which followed

161, 162. Jonathan King's "Fancy Valentine Shop", 304 Essex Road, Islington, and a photograph of girls in the workshop. Courtesy of Carroll Alton Means, Connecticut.

King's retirement in 1905. The children had other interests. Referring to his own education, he had this to say: "I left school at about twelve years of age; being ill, my attendance had been very bad. I never got further than four pages in any schoolbook; changed school when I went again and began the same books again at page 1; never got out of A in spelling," etc. "I was in those days (1848) the acting custodian of a tobacconist's and newspaper shop—I speak of the days when a newspaper such as the *Dispatch* cost sixpence, and paid stamp duty." "My wages amounted to a penny per week, paid me on Sunday afternoon. This was called 'pocket-money'— why, I cannot tell, for it never remained there."

Jonathan King was a devout man through life. When

he began business he determined never to open his shop on Sundays. He was told he would soon be ruined, and, indeed, the loss must have been great, when it is considered that in those times in his neighbourhood Sunday was the busiest day of the week. He was also a staunch teetotaller, but nullified this by being an immoderate smoker of cigars. He never took holidays, the sole exception was one at the seaside, when he got so inexpressibly bored that he returned after a few days.

"He was tall, broad-shouldered, and handsome; an indefatigable worker, making up his mind instantly. If he had started life as a soldier, he had the qualities in him to have become a general." (Ralph Thomas, *Notes & Queries*.)

In 1911 King began to worry about the future of his great collection. He realised that no ordinary collector could assume responsibility for fifteen tons of material. He took his problem to the Print Room of the British Museum and offered to sell the collection. They had no money! He then offered to give the collection outright. They had no room! He finally offered the best parts of the collection, which could be selected at will. The offer was declined! Fortunately the London Museum expressed willingness to accept part of the collection.

In April 1912 the "collector *par excellence*" passed to his reward. The bulk of his great collection remained in the rooms provided for them at 302 Essex Road. England became involved in World War I. In 1918 a mysterious fire broke out among the albums and a large number, containing Christmas cards, were destroyed. This gave rise to the legend that the entire collection had been destroyed by a German bomb.

In 1923 the collection was visited by a reporter for *The Evening News*. He wrote, "In a grey street in Islington is a shrine of old and forgotten loves. It is a weather-beaten brick house on which in faded lettering is the inscription, 'Fancy Valentines and Verse Sachets', and to it on Saint Valentine's Eve phantom lovers pay a romantic pilgrimage." He then described the "thirty or forty thousand valentines—gathered in those rooms of love's longing".

The year 1928 arrived and a selection of valentine volumes was sent to the London Museum. Quantities of rare and costly steel dies, used in the manufacture of lace-paper, were disposed of as scrap metal. The balance of the collection, now reduced in size, was sold to a London bookseller, Robert Sprange Frampton, who had

it removed to a warehouse in Durham Road. Mr. Frampton offered 90 volumes from the collection in his book catalogue (52) for Christmas and New Year, 1928-29. He offered 55 more volumes in 1930. The average asked for these volumes was about $2. In October 1930, Mr. Frampton died.

The business passed to Bartol Robert Frampton, whose interest was fishing books. Most of the collection lay in the warehouse during his active business life, but part, in his home at 4 Warwick Gardens, Harringay, was damaged by a German "buzz-bomb" in 1944. In 1947 B. R. Frampton died.

Ten years ago, renewed interest in valentines and greeting cards brought the remainder of the King collection into the market. The bulk of it was purchased by the writer [Carroll Alton Means] and it is now part of the 'Hallmark Historical Collection'. An addition of some 35 albums was made in 1958. This brings the total to more than 100 volumes, which is undoubtedly the largest concentration of albums from the King collection anywhere in the world.

Some of King's material is now on exhibition at the London Museum—and a writer in the *Sunday Times* deplored the fact that so much of the collection was allowed to cross the ocean.

APPENDIX V

EUGENE RIMMEL, 96 STRAND

Anyone walking down the Strand today might stop for a moment when passing Woolworths to reflect on the number of famous houses which formerly stood near this site. Here stood in olden times the residence of the Bishop of Carlisle, which was later converted into the town mansion of the Earls of Worcester, and called Worcester House. Afterwards, as the residence of the Duke of Beaufort it became Beaufort House, and then during the 18th century, from being a nobleman's palace it changed into a block of business premises and took the name of Beaufort Buildings. It was here that Fielding lived when he wrote *Tom Jones* and was dunned by the tax collectors for not being able to pay his taxes. Sometime in the 1820s the place was again known as Beaufort House, and was occupied by the firm of Whiting and Branston, who carried on a business of embossers and high-class engravers. Charles Whiting's name is remembered today by postal historians for the many fine entries he submitted as designs for the proposed prepayment of postage when Rowland Hill's plan for a uniform penny post was considered in 1839. By 1830 Rudolph Ackermann, the printseller, had moved from No. 101 Strand, to a shop in Beaufort House, No. 96. Ackermann, both father and son, became well known for their prints and fancy stationery and carried on business, too, at 191 Regent Street.

In the 1860s No. 96 had become the emporium of M. Eugene Rimmel, the perfumer, who specialised also in novelty valentines. *The Graphic* of February 12, 1870, had this to say of Rimmel's:

> . . . The secret must be that Mr. Rimmel's shop is St. Valentine's head-quarters. From thence proceed those elaborate devices of all hues and scents, those doves, and hearts, and darts, and floral complications, which attract gazers to the window and perfume the whole street. Perhaps if we were to penetrate into the recesses of the shop we should find a shrine devoted to the Saint, with scented pastilles ever burning before his statue, and fountains of perfume playing all around it. At the feet of the Saint would be ranged specimens of the year's supply of valentines, from sixpence upwards. 'A few in this style, very chaste, one guinea,' might occupy the place of honour. Some such tribute is certainly due to a Saint who makes himself so useful. . . .

A few years later in 1874 *All The Year Round* carried an article describing the extraordinary nature of Rimmel's enterprise and gave a wonderful picture of the activity and business brought about by St. Valentine's Day.

> We all know that great laboratory of sweet scents and pretty sights in the Strand, whence M. Rimmel sends forth perfume by the gallon, soaps by the ton, cards and valentines by the hundred-weight; and most of us have spent our money in the tempting wares that call to us by our two senses of sight and smell to go in and buy. But we have not all had the pleasant privilege of seeing over

the manufactory, noting how the work goes on from cellar to garret in the two huge houses devoted to it; how much material is used, and how much turned out; how many hands are employed, and what kind of labour they do; thus forming some estimate of the extent and importance of the business. This pleasure was accorded to the writer of these lines one afternoon shortly before St. Valentine's day, when every room that could be spared in both houses was given up to these oftentimes useful and always pretty and innocent, sweet-scented acts of commemoration by which the memory of the sainted bishop is kept alive, and the faces of the young made glad by the same.

Valentines everywhere! of all sorts and sizes, of all prices and for all purposes; from the child's penny card, with its pretty posy of roses and lilies in the middle and the quaint little love-legend beneath, to rich lace fans, pearl-handled and jewelled, worth ten pounds and more; from the scented paper sachet, with doves or flying cupids caged within a gold or silver border, or veiled beneath a covering of gauze, to a velvet glove-case, discoursing sweet music when opened; being a glove-case in intention and a musical box in fact. It would almost seem as if the

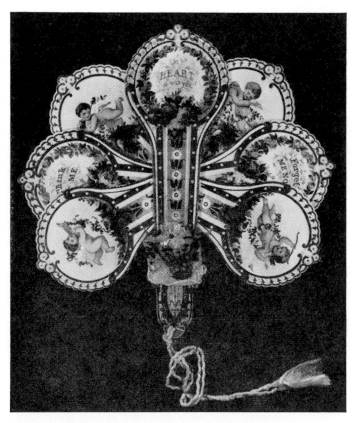

163. A delightful fan valentine by Rimmel, gaily printed in colour; the whole folds into the centrepiece. Courtesy of Robert A. Smith, Bath.

164. A valentine by Rimmel on paper made by Meek. The geraniums are made of cambric and were probably perfumed. Author's Collection.

whole valentine-sending world must surely be supplied from this one centre. There can be no room left for others! What within the list of ladies' requirements cannot be found here? Not to speak of the valentine pure and simple, the "animated flowers", the "love's photograph",—which is simply a mirror under lifting flowers —the doves that carry letters, the bouquets that mean as much as an essay, the mere prettiness without more intention than to be pretty, we have here gloves and brooches, and fans of all designs from the inexpensive flower-fan, which, when shut is a beautiful bouquet, when open a serviceable fan, to the ten-guinea Watteau picture; we have golden charms and satin neckties; head-dresses of feathers, of ribbon, of Brazilian feather-flowers, of marine flowers from Trebizonde—let us hope not with the fatal effects of that other produce of Trebizonde of which Moore speaks:

> Even as those bees of Trebizonde,
> Which from the sunniest flowers that glad
> With their pure smile the gardens round,
> Draw venom forth that drives men mad!

—or, if making men mad, then only in that perfunctory way which is called mad with love or admiration. But beside these we have also Japanese ornamental hair-pins as well as Japanese brooches, Indian jewellery, Genoese silver filagree, gold lockets and bracelets, rings and crosses, Bohemian garnets, orient pearls, topazes, turquoises and the like, to any extent. These "practical valentines" are real gifts wherein the sender shows his taste, discretion, and liberality.

It was pleasant to see the crowds of happy-looking girls working at their delicate trade. Here was one gumming round to the pictured foundation the plaited paper hinges by which the pierced outer cover is raised, preparatory to fastening on that glittering lace-like outer cover itself; here was another handling a dainty square of white satin or moiré silk, with the flowers and figures painted by hand, and cunningly painted too. Her companion to the one side was manipulating a bunch of feather flowers, she to the other was sewing on pearls or ribbon bows, as the pattern demanded. A rosy-cheeked, brown-haired girl was peeping at her own bright eyes, while securing the little square of mirror that made the photograph already spoken of; and all looked amused and interested in their work; a band of one hundred and fifty contented and well-to-do young women, nicely dressed and nicely mannered. We fancy they could scarcely be otherwise than contented and well-to-do, under the kind and genial management of that famous house, the first, we believe, to employ women at all in the manufacture of perfumery. A house, famous indeed in more senses than one; for one of the two in which M. Rimmel carries on his business was that of the Duke of Beaufort—"Beaufort House," which the conductors, and some of the contributors too of *All the Year Round* knew something of a few years ago.

It was treading familiar ground to go up and down the well-worn stairs, and over the old rooms which had once been filled with papers and presses, compositors, turnovers, and devils, type and sticks and formes and leads, and where the scramble had been among pie and pica, sanserifs and bourgeois, slanting italics and square romans. Now there are gallons of scent and miles of soap; rooms full of fancy boxes, to hold so many tablets or so many bottles—full of thin wooden boxes, to hold so many fancy boxes—full of stout and serviceable packing cases, to hold so many thin wooden boxes; packing cases set as close as building bricks, and directed to all parts of the habitable world, from Monte Video to Calabria, from Faroe to the Fiji Islands, and from Russia to Jamaicia.

ENGLISH AND AMERICAN VALENTINE MANUFACTURERS

The following lists of publishers and manufacturers' names and addresses are by no means complete. In many cases information is scanty, and, as firms frequently amalgamated and changed addresses it is difficult to date them with accuracy. They are given only as a reference in order to help collectors where possible.

VALENTINE MANUFACTURERS AND PUBLISHERS IN LONDON

Rudolph ACKERMANN	101, then in 1830 at 96, Strand. Print seller. Early 1800s.
Rudolph ACKERMANN, Jnr.	191 Regent St. Fancy stationery, print seller and valentines. 1830s onwards.
Arthur ACKERMANN	191 Regent St. Print seller. Agent for Louis Prang of Boston, Mass.
Joseph ADDENBROOKE	101 Hatton Garden, E.C. Later at Bartletts Bldg., Holborn. Invented method of lace-paper making. Early 1840s-60s.
BENBOW & Son	12 Little Britain, E.C. Perfumed sachets in form of fancy valentines. 1860s.
Edward BOLLANS & Co.	St. Brides St., E.C. Perfumed sachets and fan valentines. 1860s.
BOWLES	224 High Holborn. Movables. 1850s.
T. H. BURKE	12 Bull Head Court, Newgate. Embosser. 1840s-50s.
Robert CANTON	Aldersgate St., E.C. Valentines—movable and comic—visiting cards and most types of greetings cards. 1860s-84.
R. CARR	Houndsditch. Valentines.
CATNACH Press	Monmouth Court, Seven Dials, Bloomsbury, from 1813-80s.
„ „	James Catnach. 1813-41.
„ „	J. Paul & Co. 1841-45.
„ „	Ann Ryle & Co. 1845-59.
CATNACH PRESS (cont.)	W. S. Fortey. 1859-80s. Song sheets, street ballads, broadsheets, valentines, etc.
A. CORTMAN	Valentine maker. Late 1840s.
COX	Probably a London maker, address not known. 1850-60.
Thos. DE LA RUE	Bunhill Row. Established 1835.
DEAN & MUNDAY	35 Threadneedle St., E.C. Early 1830s. Then, Thos. Dean & Son. Later 160a Fleet St. 1850s-1900. Animated cards, comic valentines, etc.
H. DOBBS & Co.	8 New Bridge St. Established 1803.
DOBBS, BAILEY & Co.	In the 1840s at 134 Fleet St. and 13 Soho Sq. then, as
DOBBS, KIDD & Co.	Early 1850s-early 1890s. Embossers, lace-paper makers, fancy stationers.
W. H. ELLIOTT	Bucklersbury, E.C. Valentine maker; said to be the first to introduce foreign chromolithographs to replace hand colouring in 1850.
John EVANS	Cannon St. 1840s.
Thos. GOODE	In the 1830s-60s.
GOODE Bros.	Clerkenwell Green. Embossers and lace-paper makers. 1860-90s.
Alfred GRAY	London. Artist and publisher. Designed many pictorial envelopes and note-paper. Drew and published his own valentines and those of Harry Furniss. 1880-90s.
J. HARWOOD	Fenchurch St. Published pictorial writing paper and valentines. 1830s-50s.
G. INGRAM	41 Old St., E.C. Small embossed and lacy valentines. 1860s.
Jonathan KING, Snr.	45 Chapel St., Somerstown. 1845-53. Then in Seymour St., Euston Sq., until the 1860s.
Jonathan KING, Jnr.	In business at 22 Stevenson Terrace, later 295 Caledonian Rd. in 1861. Then at 304 Essex Rd., Islington, under name of E. E. King from 1872 to 1912. Fancy stationers, valentine and greetings card manufacturer.
George KERSHAW & Son	17 Wilderness Row, London. Embossed and lace-paper maker. 1840-60.
Le BLOND & Co.	24 Budge Row, Cheapside. Then to Kingston-on-Thames. One of the principal Baxter licencees; produced attractive colour prints for Rimmel, etc. 1840s to 1860s.

LLOYD Bros.	22 Ludgate Hill. Print sellers and publishers. 1850s.
Edward LLOYD	12 Salisbury Sq., Fleet St. Comic valentines. Also at 231 Shoreditch. 1840s-60s.
LONDON LACE PAPER and VALENTINE CO. (J. T. Wood & Co.) 278-280 Strand.	
Joseph MANSELL	35 Red Lion Sq. Fancy stationers. 1835. Embossers, and lace-paper makers, early valentine makers. 1840-60s.
Albert MARKS	22 Jewin St., E.C.; comic valentines. 1870s.
J. L. MARKS	23 Russell Court, Covent Garden. Early comic valentines and lithographs. 1860s.
S. MARKS & Sons	60 Gt. Prescot St., Goodman Fields. Comic valentines. 1850s.
George MEEK	Crane Court, Fleet St. Embosser and lace-paper maker. ?1840s-90s.
David MOSSMAN	Islington, London. Embossers and lace-paper makers. 1825-1901.
Mrs. MOSSMAN	1a Stoke Newington Green. Lace-paper makers, and makers of leaves and ornaments for valentines. 1865.
MULLORD Bros.	1 and 2 Penn St., N.1. Embossers and valentine makers. 1840s-70s.
Ernest NISTER	24 St. Bride St., E.C. Lithographers. A branch of Nister of Nuremburg. 1880s.
A. PARK	47 Leonard St., Finsbury. Comic valentines; woodcuts and lithographs. 1840s.
J. V. QUICK	Sutton Garden, Chalk Road, Islington. 1850s.
Eugene RIMMEL	96 Strand, 128 Regent St., and 24 Cornhill. Perfumed sachets and fancy valentines. 1860-90s.
ROCK Bros.	11 Walbrook, E.C. Pictorial writing paper and valentines. 1840s-60s.
H. A. SANDERS	Fleet St., E.C. Lace-paper makers and valentines. 1840s-50s.
G. SMEETON	74 Tooley Street, Bermondsey.
Thos. STEVENS (of Coventry)	114 Newgate St., E.C. Woven silk centres and sachets for valentines; woven silk bookmarkers. 1860s.
Benjamin SULMAN	177 Upper Thames St. Later in City Rd. and Warwick Lane. Small embossed valentines and sachets. 1860s.
TOROND	4 West St., Soho. Cheap comic valentines. c. 1830s-40s.

Raphael TUCK	Published chromolithograph valentines in 1881, under the name of Raphael Tuck & Sons, Coleman St., E.C. Established 1866.
Marcus WARD & Co.	London and Belfast. Published valentines by Kate Greenaway and Walter Crane. 1866-98.
WESTWOOD	Not found in the London directories. Embosser and valentine maker. Early 1830s.
John WINDSOR & Sons	Clerkenwell. Embosser. 1840-50s.
J. T. WOOD & Co.	278-280 Strand. Embosser and lace-paper maker, comic valentines. Also known as London Lace Paper & Valentine Company. 1840s-70s.

Jonathan King listed the principal valentine makers who were in business about the year 1880 to be:

Atterton; Brown; Bollans; Canton; Carr & Mason; Dobbs, Kidd & Co.; Dean; Easton; Goode Bros.; Howes; Haynes; Hurst & Pridham; Ingram; J. King; Love; Mansell; Mullord; Marcus Ward; Mitchell; Mead; Mossman; T. Meek; W. J. Meek; Robertson; Rimmel; T. Stevens; Sulman; Turner; Walker & Sons; Wood; Wright; and Windsor.

OTHER VALENTINE PUBLISHERS AND MAKERS

W. & A. M'FARLANE	333 Sauchiehall St., Glasgow.
Bartholomew F. LLOYD	Edinburgh.
James KENDREW	23 Colliergate, York. 1820-30s.
RICHARDSON & Son	Derby. 1840-50s.
J. ROBEY & Sons	Leamington. 1859-69.
J. ROBINSON	Glasgow.
T. STEVENS	Coventry. Woven silk specialties. 1860s-70s.
WELCH & LENTON	Coventry. Woven silk specialties. 1860s-70s.
J. WRIGLEY	25 Miller St., Manchester.

AMERICAN PUBLISHERS AND VALENTINE MAKERS

AMERICAN VALENTINE COMPANY	165 William St. and 14 Chambers St., New York. 1860s.
J. ANDREWS	38 Chatham St. Published civil war and patriotic valentines, song sheets, etc.
BALDWIN & GLEASON	Boston. Published small valentines on ivorine. 1880.
BERLIN & JONES	New York. 1850-60s. Taken over by George C. Whitney Co. in 1869.

BULLARD ART PUBLISHING CO.	Worcester, Mass. 1887. Taken over by George C. Whitney Co.
CALDWELL	In business as Caldwell & Co., 82 Cedar St., New York, in 1865.
Philip J. COZANS	107 Nassau St., New York, later joined HUESTIS, to become HUESTIS and COZANS at 104 Nassau St. 1850-62.
Pasqual DONALDSON	178 Orchard Street, New York. 1839-55.
George DUNN	Richmond, Va. Civil war and patriotic valentines. 1860s.
ELTON (Robert H. & Co.)	New York. Engraver. Started business about 1834 as ELTONS, 98 Nassau St.; relinquished this address to T. W. STRONG in 1844 and moved to Division St. Also known as ELTON & Co. In 1846 claimed to be the first designer of valentines in the country. Eventually sold out to McLoughlin Bros.
Abraham FISHER	74 Chatham Sq., New York. Also in Philadelphia. Associated as TURNER & FISHER, and then FISHER & Brothers, FISHER & DENISON, A. J. FISHER. A. J. FISHER was at 98 Nassau St. in 1874 (according to catalogues and sales lists of that date). Claimed to be the oldest valentine house in America since 1834. This was Elton's date at this address. 1836-60.
T. FRERE	83 Nassau St., New York. 1850s.
G. S. HASKINS & Company	36 Beekman St., New York. Civil war valentines. 1861-63.
HOWLAND, S. A.	(Southworth Allen) father of Esther Allen Howland. Bookbinder and fancy stationer in Worcester, Mass. Of his five children Esther was the only daughter. 1842-52.
Esther HOWLAND	16 Summer St. and 425 Main St., Worcester, Mass. Also known as the New England Valentine Company. 1849-81.
Charles P. HUESTIS	Engraver. 104 Nassau St. (corner of Ann St.), New York, as noted in the 1846 New York Directory. Published a *Valentine Writer* in 1846. 1841-53.
McLOUGHLIN Bros.	New York. Took over the comic valentine business of Eltons. Also published paper dolls, juvenile books and games. 1848-1950.
Charles MAGNUS	12 Frankfurt St., New York. Well known for pictorial headed writing paper and envelopes; also for civil war and patriotic stationery and valentines. 1854-70.
Richard MARSH	New York. Published valentines in the form of bank-notes, etc. 1850-54.
De MARSAN H.	Publisher. 38 Chatham Sq., New York. Not mentioned in the 1846 Directory. He succeeded J. Andrews, publisher, continuing same line: song sheets, toy books, paper dolls, etc.
NEW ENGLAND VALENTINE CO.	(Esther Howland.) 16 Summer St., and 425 Main St., Worcester, Mass.
NEW YORK UNION VALENTINE Company	134 William St., New York.
Louis PRANG	Boston. 1867-89.
OBPACHER	New York. Branch of Obpacher, Munich. 1880s.
George SNYDER	In 1845 at 112 John St., New York. Lithographer: 1846-47 at 122 Fulton St., then at various addresses in the same district until 1857-92, at 92 William St.
T. W. STRONG	153 Fulton St. and 98 Nassau St., New York. 1842-69.
Jotham TAFT	Worcester, Mass. Worked at times on his own as valentine maker. Also worked for Esther Howland and finally for Berlin & Jones. 1860s-89.
Edward TAFT, son of Jotham.	Also worked for Esther Howland. 1879-89.
Fred TURNER	Philadelphia. Then as Turner and Fisher. Also at 74 Chatham Sq., New York. Eventually sold out to George C. Whitney. 1843-50.
Edward A. WHAITES	1 Courthan St. and 347 Broadway, New York. 1836-68.
GEORGE C. WHITNEY Company	Worcester, Mass. 1866-1942.
WHITNEY Brothers	
WHITNEY Manufacturing Company	
James WRIGLEY	273½ Division St., New York, then as publisher, first at 27 Chatham St., later at 61 Chatham St., New York. 1846-70.

VALENTINE PRICES

The lists shown in the illustrations give a reasonable idea of the cost of Valentines, for, as prices were stable in those days, it can be conjectured that these sort of prices prevailed more or less throughout the Victorian era. Jonathan King was a great believer in publicity and printed a vast amount of price lists and 'hand-outs'. Fortunately some of this ephemera has survived, and, as he was one of the popular valentine makers, catering for all tastes, his prices can be regarded as normal for those days; the illustrations of his price lists are dated for 1863 and will be of value to the historian, particularly as everything is described in detail.

High-class establishments such as Mansell and Rimmel offered their more extravagant 'creations' priced in guineas, and it was possible to pay up to £25 for a single valentine; but of course such instances were exceptional.

The price list of A. J. Fisher (illustrated on page 140), the well-known valentine maker of 98 Nassau Street, New York, has been selected as being fairly representative of the majority of American valentine manufacturers. However, specially made valentines and valentines desired for the luxury trade could cost up to $50 apiece.

J. KING,
WHOLESALE MANUFACTURER OF FANCY FLORAL VALENTINES,
Scent Packets, Book Marks, Needle Books, Verse Cards,
AND VALENTINE ORNAMENTS,
56, SEYMOUR STREET,
EUSTON SQUARE, LONDON, N.W.

LIST OF PRICES OF VALENTINES.
14 as 12—a variety in each dozen.

NO.	SIZE.	DESCRIPTION.	Per Gross.	Intended to sell at each.
1	64mo.	Gold Paper	8/	1d.
2	32mo.	White do.	8/	1d.
3	,,	Tinted do.	14/	2d.
4	64mo.	Gold do. Raised, to lift up	14/	2d.
5	32mo.	Gold do.	21/	3d.
6	Hearts	Ditto Raised	21/	3d.
6LY.	Queen's	Silver do. Silk Centres	36/	6d.
7	Shields		21/	3d.
8	Diamond	Tinted do.	1/10	3d.
O 9	,,	White do. Flowers Painted on Rice Paper	14/	2d.
9	Diamond	Gold do. For Children	28/	4d.
10	Queen's	Tinted do. Ditto	28/	4d.
			Per Doz.	
10LY.	Diamond		3/	6d.
11	Silk Bags	Scented (each in a separate box)	3/9	6d.
12	Envelopes	Gold do.	3/6	6d.
13	Hearts	To lift up, with a verse under	3/6	6d.
14	Diamond	Gold do. Raised (very cheap)	3/6	6d.
14H	Heart	Silver do. Questions and Answers	3/6	6d.
14LY.	Queen's	(A Job Lot)	3/	6d.
15	Diamond	With a Brooch or Charm	3/9	6d.
15 LY.	Diamond	Tinted do. { With a Book Mark, which can be removed without injuring the Valentine and a Brooch substituted }	3/6	6d.
16	8vo.	White do. Advertisements, Love Letters, &c.	3/6	6d.
17	Diamond	Quite new, Pusseys	3/6	6d.
17LY.	8vo.	White do. Apple Sauce	3/6	6d.
O 17LY.	Queen's	Silver do. FROM Parents and Friends	4/	6d.

NO.	SIZE.	DESCRIPTION.	Per Gross.	Intended to sell at each.
18	Queen's ....Gold Paper	Various	3/3	6d.
18LY.	8vo. ....Silver do.	Odd Patterns (very cheap)	5/3	9d.
19	Queen's ....Gold do.		3/	6d.
19LY.	Square 8vo..Silver do.		7/	1/
20	Albert ....Tinted do.	Various	3/6	6d.
O 20LY.	8vo. ....Plain do.	Painted on Rice Paper	3/6	6d.
21	Envelope .....Tinted do.	Frosted	3/6	6d.
21LY.	Envelopes...Silver do.	{ Paper Collars & Satin Necktips (a novelty) each Valentine in a Box }	7/	1/
22	Diamond ......Gold do.	Frosted	3/6	6d.
22LY.	Queen's ... Ditto	{ With Lace Blond round, each Valentine in a Box }	7/	1/
23	8vo.	Large Flowers with Verse under.	3/6	6d.
24	„ ....White do.	Bird Nests, and Moss with written words	3/6	6d.
25	„	Gloves on a Valentine	3/6	6d.
26	„	(After the style of 14 Queen's)...	3/6	6d.
27	„ ....Gold do.	No Fly Leaf	3/6	6d.
O 27	Diamond	Each Valentine in a Gilt Edge Cabinet Box..	10/6	1/6
28	8vo. ....Gold do.	Gelatine Centre	3/6	6d.
O 28LY.	Large 8vo.. Ditto	{ A Book Mark attached to the Valentine, which can be removed and used, leaving the Valentine still perfect }	14/	2/
29LY.	8vo. .... Ditto	With Church, the doors to open...	10/6	1/6
31	8vo. ....Silver do.	Large Rice Centre	7/	1/
32	„ .... Ditto	Three sheets of paper, very cheap.	7/	1/
33	„ ....Gold do.	Jewelled	7/	1/
33LY.	„ ....White do.	Satin Book Mark	14/	2/
34	„ ....Gold do.	With Blond, Raised	7/	1/
35	„ ...... Ditto	Raised	7/	1/
36	„ .... Ditto	Ditto	7/	1/
36LY.	„ ....Gold do.	Cupid's Pocket Book	14/	2/
37	„ ...... Ditto	Large piece of Silk with Boquet of Flowers	7/	1/
38	„ ...... Ditto	Raised	10/6	1/6
				Boxed in dozens.
38LY.	Very small 4to. Silver	Very cheap, boxed seperately	17/6	2/6
39	„ .... Ditto	Pretty	10/6	1/6
39LY.	„ .... Ditto	Cupid's Dream (novelty)	24/	3/
O 39LY.	Large 8vo.. Ditto	Painted Mottoes	17/6	2/6
40	8vo. .... Ditto	Large Satin Centre	10/6	1/6
41	„ .... Ditto	To raise up at each corner	10/6	1/6
41LY.	„ .... Ditto	Bird made with Feathers	21/	3/
42	Diamond ...... Ditto	Ring Envelope	10/6	1/6
43	8vo. ....White do.	Very chaste and cheap	14/	2/
43LY.	„ ....Silver do.	"Love and a Cottage is all I ask".	28/	4/
44	„ ....Gold do.	Cupid's Card Rack	14/	2/
44LY.	„ .... Ditto	Cork View and Basket	28/	4/
45	8vo. ....Silver Paper	Love in a Cottage	14/	2/
O 45LY.	„ .... Ditto	Shells, &c.	28/	4/
45LY.	„ .... Ditto	Perfumed Centre worked with needle	28/	4/
46	„ ....Gold do.	Blond round, Silver Centre	14/	2/
46LY.	„ ....Silver do.	Pearl Centre Ornament	28/	4/
47	„ .... Ditto	Blond round, Satin Centre	14/	2/
				Each Valentine in a separate box.
47LY.	„	Elaborate	35/	5/
48	„ ....Tinted Gold do.	Artificial Flowers ...	17/6	2/6
49	„ ....Silver do.	Chaste	17/6	2/6
50	„ .... Ditto	Bird and Weed	17/6	2/6
O 50LY.	Large 8vo.. Ditto	Sea Weed and View	28/	4/
51	8vo. .... Ditto	Basket of Flower	17/6	2/6
51LY.	„ .... Ditto	Love's Railway	28/	4/
52	Queen's ... .. Ditto	Elaborate	21/	3/
53	„ .... Ditto	Neat	21/	3/
53LY.	Large 8vo. ... Ditto	Anchor of Hope	28/	4/
54	8vo. .... Ditto	Very soft and light	21/	3/
55	„ .... Ditto	German style	21/	3/
56	„ .... Ditto	White Lilies, very light	28/	4/
57	„ .... Ditto	Thick Wreath of Flowers	28/	4/
58	8vo. .... Ditto		28/	4/
59	8vo. .... Ditto	Quiet, but very pretty	21/	3/
60	„ .... Ditto	Beautifully Painted on Rice Paper	35/	5/
61	„ .... Ditto	Ditto, with Lilies round	35/	5/
62	„ .... Ditto	{ Photograph Marriage, with Wreath of Orange Blossoms round }	35/	5/
63	„ ....White do.	Lily, Wreath, &c...	35/	5/
64	„ ....Silver do.	Double Silver Paper, elaborate	35/	5/
65	„ .... Ditto	Rice Paper, Pearl Beads, &c...	42/	6/
65 Extra	„ .... Ditto	{ Ditto ditto, with Ivory Painting, very pretty }	54/	7/6
66	„ ...... Ditto	Sideways, sweetly pretty	42/	6/
67	8vo. .... Ditto	Figure made with Rice Paper	42/	6/
68	Diamond ...... Ditto	Extra Patterns, with Ivory, &c...	21/	3/
70	8vo. .... Ditto	After the style of No. 66	42/	6/
71	„ .... Ditto	{ Love in a Cottage, &c., very nicely worked up }	42/	6/
72	„ .... Ditto	Ivory Figures, &c.	54/	7/6
74	„ .... Ditto	{ Love's Bark, a small Compass, with words appropriate }	42/	6/
75	„ .... Ditto	Photograph Figures, Cupid, &c...	42/	6/
76	„ .... Ditto	Sideways, with Wreath of Artificial Flowers	35/	5/
77	„ .... Ditto	{ Beautifully made, Heartsease Wreath, Pearl Beads, &c. }	54/	7/6
78	„ .... Ditto	"Keep this in Remembrance of me"	35/	5/
79	„ .... Ditto	{ After the style of No. 65, only with Ivory Painting }	54/	7/6

Courtesy of the London Museum

THE OLDEST VALENTINE HOUSE IN AMERICA.

Valentines for 1874.

QUALITY IMPROVED! PRICES REDUCED!

The reputation of this house for **40** years—of making the most saleable Valentine stock—will be maintained in the line *now ready* for the approaching season.

This stock is assorted to suit the dealer's trade,

IN LOTS.

Each lot is a complete assortment, and contains *four and one-fourth times* its cost in Retail Valentines.

$2.50 Lot, Complete Assortment, retails for				**$10.75**
5.00 "	"	"	"	21.44
10.00 "	"	"	"	42.88
20.00 "	"	"	"	85.76
25.00 "	"	"	"	107.20

Examine Contents of Lots on Next Page.

EACH LOT CONTAINS 1 GROSS OF COMIC VALENTINES FOR EVERY $5.00.

Customers are at liberty to change the contents of lots to suit themselves,

but the proportions in these lots are believed to be the best that can be made.

My assortment of 8 numbers of Comic Valentines includes

THREE NEW SERIES OF COMICS.

I claim to sell

The Best and Cheapest Stock,
The Brightest and most Tasteful Designs,

and to FILL all Orders on the day of receipt.

The establishment of this house since 1834—a period of 40 years—is a guarantee to new customers that they will be liberally, promptly and honestly dealt with.

A. J. FISHER, 98 Nassau Street, N. Y.

Twenty Dollar Lot.

RETAILS FOR $85.76.

Price by Mail, $21.30.

75 VALENTINES,	at	5 cts.	$3.75
60 "	"	10 "	6.00
48 "	"	15 "	7.20
40 "	"	25 "	10.00
25 "	"	35 "	8.75
20 "	"	50 "	10.00
10 "	"	75 "	7.50
6 "	"	1,00 "	6.00
3 "	"	2,00 "	6.00
1 "	"	3.00 "	3.00
50 " CARDS, Gilt,	10 "	5.00
175 " ENVELOPES,	2 "	3.50
60 " "	3 "	1.80
30 " "	5 "	1.50
			$80.00
4 Gross Comic Valentines,	1 cent	5.76
HANDSOME SHOW CARDS.		$85.76

Postage 1.30

Packed for Express, in wood cases,

Twenty-five Dollar Lot.

RETAILS FOR $107.20.

Price by Mail, $26.70.

100 VALENTINES,	at	5 cts.	$5.00
89 "	"	10 "	8.90
67 "	"	15 "	10.05
48 "	"	25 "	12.00
30 "	"	35 "	10.50
24 "	"	50 "	12.00
12 "	"	75 "	9.00
6 "	"	1,00 "	6.00
3 "	"	2.00 "	6.00
2 "	"	3.00 "	6.00
60 " CARDS, Gilt,	10 "	6.00
225 " ENVELOPES,	2 "	4.50
75 " "	3 "	2.25
35 " "	5 "	1.75
			$100.00
5 Gross Comic Valentines,	1 cent	7.20
HANDSOME SHOW CARDS.		$107.20

Postage 1.70

Packed for Express, in wood cases,

Courtesy of Hallmark Historical Collection

BIBLIOGRAPHY

Hone's Every Day Book, 1826 and 1827. Reprinted by Ward Lock, 1889

Hone's Year Book, 1832. Reprinted by Ward Lock

St. Valentine's Day and Valentines. W. H. Cremer, Jnr. Cremer, London, 1870

In Praise of Bishop Valentine. Frank E. Bliss. Privately printed 1893

Kate Greenaway. M. H. Spielman & G. S. Layard. Black, 1905

Les Valentines et La Saint-Valentin. Laure-Paul Flobert. Lefebure-Durocq, Lille, 1912

Das Kleine Andachtsbild vom XIV bis zum XX Jahrhundert. Adolf Spamer, Munich, 1930

The History of Valentines. Ruth Webb Lee. Batsford, 1953

The History of the Christmas Card. George Buday, Rockcliff, 1954

The Fraktur Writings or Illuminated Manuscripts of the Pennsylvania Germans. Donald A. Shelly. Pennsylvania German Folklore Society, 1960

Oxford Dictionary of Nursery Rhymes. Opie. O.U.P., 1966

The Picture Postcard and its Origins. Frank Staff. Lutterworth, 1966

Articles

Cupid's Manufactory. *All the Year Round*. Feb. 20, 1864

From Gay to Grave. *All the Year Round*, March 21, 1874

St. Valentine's Day. Prof. John W. Hales. *The Antiquary*, Feb. 1882

The Vanishing Valentine. W. G. Fitzgerald. *Strand Magazine*, 1895

Biedermeier Wuensche. Gustav E. Pazaurek. *Mitteillungen des Nord-Boehmischen Gewerbemuseums*, 1905

The Painswick Feast: Its Origin and Meaning. Rev. W. H. Seddon. 1921

Kate Greenaway's Valentines. Carroll Alton Means. *Hobbies* (Chicago, Ill.), Feb.-July, 1953

INDEX

The numerals in bold refer to illustration numbers